WORD UNHEARD

A Guide through Eliot's *Four Quartets*

WORD UNHEARD

*A Guide through Eliot's
Four Quartets*

by HARRY BLAMIRES

METHUEN & CO LTD
11 NEW FETTER LANE LONDON EC4

First published 1969 by
Methuen & Co. Ltd,
11 New Fetter Lane London EC4
© 1969 by Harry Blamires
Printed in Great Britain by
Richard Clay (The Chaucer Press), Ltd,
Bungay, Suffolk
1·1
416 14020 3/35   416 29910 5/49

DISTRIBUTED IN THE USA BY
BARNES AND NOBLE INC

CONTENTS

INTRODUCTORY NOTE   I

Burnt Norton   7

East Coker   41

The Dry Salvages   79

Little Gidding   123

APPENDIX I   185

APPENDIX II   190

APPENDIX III   193

INDEX   197

ACKNOWLEDGEMENTS

T. S. Eliot's *Four Quartets* is published by Faber and Faber (London) and Harcourt Brace (New York) to whom grateful acknowledgement is made for the use of all quotations. References in the text are to line numbers of each section of the poem.

I should like to record my thanks and indebtedness to Dr Harold Brooks for his help and advice.

I share the general indebtedness of Eliot's readers and critics to the pioneer work of Helen Gardner, Elizabeth Drew, Raymond Preston, and Grover Smith.

'The communication
Of the dead is tongued with fire beyond the language of the living'

LITTLE GIDDING

INTRODUCTORY NOTE

I have wanted to write this book ever since the time of Eliot's death, when I read a tribute to Eliot by a distinguished critic, who observed that *Four Quartets* is a poem which only a highly trained philosopher could understand. I do not think Eliot wrote anything exclusively for highly trained philosophers, but I think he was himself acutely sensitive to the ironical situation in which the work of a poet richly nourished on literary and theological orthodoxies, could be assumed to be material fit for learned specialists rather than for the general reading public.

On the basis of the accepted difficulty of the poem, the plan and purpose of the present book explain themselves. The reader is guided through *Four Quartets* movement by movement, indeed line by line, by a continuous elucidation which blends paraphrase with commentary, and relies on frequent cross-reference in the process of clarifying and filling out the 'meaning'. I have tried to stick closely to Eliot's rhythm of presentation, but all readers of *Four Quartets* must be aware that, as one proceeds through the poem as a whole, allusions, images, and arguments continually throw back needful further illumination on what has already been said. The throwback of meaning and the forecasting of meaning are as consistently natural to the poetic practice of Eliot in *Four Quartets* as they are to that of Joyce in *Ulysses*. It follows that the commentator cannot have his say about any given passage and then mentally tick it off as he moves on to the next. The guide must occasionally anticipate what has yet to be said by the poet, and he must often go back to passages already dealt with, in order to complete their elucidation. This is an especial necessity in the case of *Burnt Norton*. The reader must not on any account conclude that at the end of the chapter on *Burnt Norton* he has heard what this book has to say about the first Quartet. He can assume that only when he has reached the last word of Appendix III.

It is no accident that a guide to *Four Quartets* should follow hard on the heels of a guide to *Ulysses*. The critic who comes to the surface after months of being submerged in Joyce inevitably looks at twentieth-century literature (and criticism) in a new light. What he sees provokes him frequently to say, 'But this won't do: it's pre-Joycean.' Very rarely, to judge from my experience, is he tempted to say of a work, 'Ah, this is surely post-Joycean!' I would place *Four Quartets* first among the works which emphatically do provoke the latter response. The influence of *Ulysses* can be detected throughout the poem. Its patterning is systematic and complex in the Joycean way, its use of words Joycean to a degree which critics (many of them largely unaware of Joyce) have scarcely begun to sense. There is an advance on the poetic technique (I use the phrase deliberately) of *Ulysses* in the sense that Eliot makes use of a new principle of referential economy, packing in not so much by what is said as by what is hinted at, something of that abundance and multiplicity of reference that Joyce achieved through the sheer weight of accumulation. *Four Quartets* is post-Joycean in that it fully reckons with the thematic development of verbal overtones which is characteristic of *Ulysses*. Joyce, I think, who not without some justice called *The Waste Land* 'an unacknowledged parody of *Ulysses*', must surely have been flattered to see Eliot turned finally into the greatest Joycean of all.

It would be interesting, though obviously outside the scope of this book, to compare *Four Quartets* with other notable instances of truly post-Joycean literature, which show both the influence of *Ulysses* and the capacity to take a step farther than Joyce. Samuel Beckett's work might be cited. In *Murphy*, *Waiting for Godot*, *Happy Days*, and the rest, the reaction against the peculiarly Joycean brand of abundance and multiplicity is as marked as it is in Eliot. But whereas Eliot's reaction against compressed accumulation in the Joycean manner is made by a principle of verbal economy that exploits the mind's capacity to follow echoes, Beckett's reaction is made according to a principle of artistic miserliness that substitutes a symbolic algebra for the teeming abundance of the living world. If Eliot's economy has a musical ancestry, Beckett's has a mathematical one. We must accept that a lady can be as effectively pinned down in a sand-dune as in the complex ritual of urbanized social life, and that for all the current paraphernalia of hygiene and vanity a tooth-brush and a hand-mirror will serve; but in accepting Beckett's imaginative equations, we sense prophetically the coming menace of the computer.

It may be helpful to say a little more, in advance of our journey through *Four Quartets*, about the verbal technique of *echoing* on which Eliot's referential system is built. That echoing is as much an aspect of the poet's meaning as of his technique will be evident to anyone who has closely studied *Four Quartets*. The poem is *about* echoes; the poem *utilizes* echoes; the poem *is* echoes. Echoes inhabit the garden, the poem, the culture of our day, the temporal world we live in; other echoes and echoes of the Other. Correspondingly the poet's words echo thus in your mind. To explain these points fully would be to investigate the meaning of the whole poem. That is the task which this book is about to attempt.

Echoes have to be attended to. Quietly one must allow the words of *Four Quartets* to resonate, for the full meaning of Eliot's key words is gathered only when one catches in a given context the overtones which the word carries from its use at other points in the poem, and may of course be further enriched when one catches overtones carried from outside the poem. Eliot's meaning and technique are blended, indeed fused, in such a way that the receptive reader of the poem, who has given it the chance to do its proper work, will be unable to read key words without catching internal reverberations (from other usages within the poem) and certain external reverberations (from other usages in literature).

The effect is to make the total experience of the poem an existential encounter with what, in loose terms, the poem might be said to be 'about'.

Thus the reader who really knows the poem will not be able to receive the word 'Footfalls' (*BN* 11) without catching a meaningful echo of the feet of the generations of dancing, breeding, and dying countrymen of *East Coker* (45), 'Feet rising and falling'. Nor will he be able to receive that word without catching overtones derived from usage of the word 'fall' at several other points in the poem – usages in which memories and echoes of other falls and Falls are eventually deeply embedded. We shall not have exhausted the packed meaning of the word even when we have fully explored the interconnectedness of its various connotations throughout the network of usages which unifies the poem and systematizes it as few works of English literature have been systematized. For the external reverberations of the word 'Footfall' come echoing back from Francis Thompson's *The Hound of Heaven* as well as from elsewhere in Eliot's own earlier work.

The form of *Four Quartets* resembles musical form in that figures and hints are transformed into articulate themes by a process of repetition and accumulation. Hints of *Hamlet*, for instance, are eventually blended in *Little Gidding* with allusions to King Charles I to form what might be called the theme of the murdered or martyred king. There are faint echoes of *Macbeth* to enrich the theme with memories of Duncan, and other shadowy royal figures hover in the background. Finally the image of the crucified King of the Jews sets another kind of crown on the little cluster.

It is perhaps only after repeated re-reading that one recognizes how fully populated the poem is. But we are told how echoes 'inhabit' the garden; we are told of 'hidden music' and concealed presences: it is our fault if we fail to find the inhabitants or hear their voices – our fault because it needs only quite a little knowledge of other literature to identify many of them. Scholarly research will not help much in opening our ears to the hidden music. It is not by research, but by listening, that one learns, for instance, in reading of 'the dull façade/And the tombstone' (*LG* 29–30) to recall the scenic 'façade' of the theatre (*EC* 117). By listening again one learns that as the 'façade' was 'rolled away' (*EC* 117) to a 'rumble of wings' (*EC* 115), so a 'tombstone' (*LG* 30) might be 'rolled away' (St Luke's words) to a rumble of angelic wings. Thus, if we listen, we come unexpectedly, behind the pigsty at Little Gidding, on the empty tomb in the garden of the Resurrection. By listening again we see how the continuing emptiness-theme (firmly linked to the image of the tombstone in *LG* 30–3, and to the minds and lives of the people around us at several points in the Quartets) blends the now recovered image of the empty tomb in the garden of the Resurrection with the empty pool in the garden of *Burnt Norton* ('and the pool was empty', *BN* 39).

At the end of all our readings and listenings we shall want to make a *schema* so that others can quickly relish the rich organization that we have gradually recognized. This is a proper and laudable desire: yet we must here resist it because we have chosen to escort the reader through the poem rather than to give him an advance blue-print of its structure. Our choice is based on the desire to let Eliot's poem do its own work in its own way. And if anyone objects that to write a guide to *Four Quartets* is a strange way of leaving the poem to do its own work, the reply must be that we do not write in a vacuum and that there is already criticism about us which is positively hindering Eliot's poetry from doing its own work. Guides become necessary when people are losing their way.

Interpretation of *Four Quartets* will not after all be easy for the highly trained philosopher as such. Rather understanding of the poem will come most naturally and easily to those readers who are prepared to be quietly receptive. And lest the reader is tempted to say that Eliot's technique has now been made to sound too complicated and contrived, we must repeat that the technique and the meaning are one and indivisible. The echoing system we have discussed is, strictly speaking, not a *device* but a mode of expression exactly matching the meaning. And even that sentence does not convey the full reality of the fusion that confronts us as we enter this poem. The existential appropriateness of *style* to *meaning* makes separation of these two terms misleading. We are not even asked, it will be noted, to *listen* to the echoes. We are told that they inhabit the garden and your mind, and we are invited to *follow*, and *find* them. Shall we follow?

If we do, we must be prepared for strange surprises as the character of Eliot's multi-dimensional allusiveness is unfolded. When his ear is fully attuned to its music, the reader of *Four Quartets* will move among words laden with the lived experience of men and women. Here he will suddenly detect in the distance the cries of those who went down one night in the *Titanic*; there he will catch a faint echo of their voices singing a hymn at the last, or hear the ship's radio tapping out its call for help. Into the pause and the silence when a train 'stops too long between stations' there will ultimately intrude the memory of a train that stopped so long between stations that it never reached its destination, and the cries of those passengers who were suddenly swept with it into the Firth of Tay. Of course no one can yet say just how much hidden music of this kind the poem contains. In the detection of meaning so multifold as Eliot's the guide can but lead the way through the foliage in which it is hidden; and he must accept that some of those who go with him may prove to have sharper ears than his own.

Burnt Norton

I

Time present and time past

Eliot first cancels out our superficial notion of time as a straight line on which we move steadily forward from the past, through the present, to the future, in a series of mutually exclusive phases. This notion is linked with various false readings of the human situation which he is later at pains to discredit. The present and the past are both perhaps 'present' in the future (that is, there, to hand, as in the usage 'I hope to be present tomorrow'), and the future is perhaps 'contained' (*BN* 3) in the past, that is to say, held back in readiness. (See *BN* 41, where the children are 'containing', holding back, their laughter.) Thus in the first three lines Eliot mentally pencils out a circle and thereby establishes an image which is to be with us through the rest of the poem (a circle within a quartet, a 'box circle', *BN* 32). He puts his finger on the present, pushes it back to the past, takes both present and past together over to the future, and then swings this laden future back to the past in which it is all 'contained'. So once again to our present at the centre of the circle. If all time is thus eternally about us ('present', *BN* 4), then all time is 'unredeemable' (*BN* 5). It cannot be recovered, recanted, bought back. The might-have-been is not a practical possibility but a purely theoretical hypothesis. The actual past and the might-have-been past are equally directed in focus towards the same point, the present, which is their 'end' (*BN* 10). The first use of the highly charged word 'end' is crucial, and line 10 is ambiguous. Actual past and might-have-been past both lead to the same conclusive present. And they both bear witness ('point') to the same purpose ('end') which is always with us ('present').

The blending of abstract and concrete, the philosophical and the experiential, is a central fact alike of Eliot's technique and of his meaning. So he moves now from abstraction to imagery, from argument to experience. He records an experience in which actual past and might-have-been past are mixed in such a way that the reader, not knowing all the details of Eliot's personal history, could not fully disentangle them. Moreover, it is an experience in which personal history and racial history, the particular and the universal, are so knit that the reader can assimilate it only as a perfect compound of the archetypal and the private. The voice speaks to him publicly as man while probing at the same time the secrets of his individual separateness. For this purpose Eliot's images, half-generalized into symbols by his repeated use of them in this poem and elsewhere, are at once loaded and exact. Footfalls sounding the tread of the unseen have earlier in Eliot's work represented the fitful incursion into human life and consciousness of reminders that beyond the walls of the familiar may lurk the impending Other. (An echo of Francis Thompson's *The Hound of Heaven* is no doubt here intended too – 'Halts by me that footfall', see p. 56). The echo of footfalls (*BN* 11) brings the first concrete realization of that possible Other, not as threatening cataclysm but as offering a revelation. The 'passage which we did not take' (the might-have-been past, *BN* 12) is the first of a series of imaged passages. We must link this one, in comparison and contrast, not only with the underground railways and overshadowed roads, but also with that 'passage' in *Little Gidding* which likewise allows movement 'Between two worlds' (*LG* 122). The rose-garden is the might-have-been dream world we never quite got inside. It is also our 'first world' (*BN* 21), the lost world of childhood innocence, and the lost paradisal Eden of humanity's unfallen condition. During the course of the poem the garden is to gather significance as the symbol of the world before the Fall. When the garden imagery recurs most fully at the end of *Little Gidding*, we learn that the children of *BN* 40 are hidden in 'the apple-tree' (*LG* 248).

Increasing familiarity with the poem leads one to believe that Eliot intentionally uses the syllable 'fall' in compound nouns so as to produce a faint, half-realized echo of the Fall. In this carefully constructed work he forms such compounds in relation to each of the four elements, earth, water, air, and fire, of which we and our world are compounded. Hence 'footfall' here, 'waterfall', (*LG* 247 and *DS* 210), 'nightfall' (*LG* 175 and *DS* 146), and 'smokefall' (*BN* 87). It scarcely needs to be said that the rose garden has its sexual significance too and that the 'passage' between two worlds is the passage through which we are born into this one and through which we try to return to a lost happiness.

But to what purpose

The poet's words, poking among the dried rose-leaves of our memories in the bowl of our minds, disturbs the dust. Thus the 'story' begins with a puff of dust, as it is to end (*LG* 56–7). Notice that the might-have-been past and the actual past have both pointed to one end, namely the present moment at which you, the reader, are reading Eliot's words. Thus the poet's 'end' in writing is truly present in the beginning of the poem and of your reading. Moreover, this present point (at which poet's past, humanity's past, and your past, actual and might-have-been, all alike meet), in which beginning and end are contained, is paragraphically separated in the centre of movement I. Around it (the image* of your bowl-like mind disturbed by the poet's echoing words) the rest of the movement revolves like a wheel, its end (the last three lines, *BN* 44–6) echoing its beginning (*BN* 1–3). Thus just as your pivotal experience now, as reader, at this moment instances that eternal central present to which past and future feed in their 'memories' (for the future too is a 'faded song, a Royal Rose', *DS* 126), so your reliving in this

---

* Later, more attuned, experience of the poem will probably enable the reader to detect in the 'dust . . . bowl' of *BN* 16 the far-off pre-echo of an allusion to the American desert more plainly evident in *LG* 66–7.

movement of an experience in the personal and archetypal
garden of actual, lost, and might-have-been delight, instances an existential now in which you are (as rarely so) fully
conscious. ('To be conscious is not to be in time,' *BN* 84.)

Although it is too soon in our encounter with the poem to
try to press upon the reader anything like the full weight of
Eliot's multi-dimensional thinking, it is important to indicate what the multi-dimensional use of words amounts to
and what a load of connotation it can carry. Thus, as
experience of the poem accumulates, the emphatic 'I do not
know' (*BN* 17) will give to the puff of dust (*BN* 16) the
character of a miniature cloud of not-knowing. This faint
hint of a Cloud of Unknowing at the still centre of the
poem's first movement becomes clearly detectable and
significant when we recognize that *The Cloud of Unknowing* is
directly quoted at the still centre of the poem's last movement (*LG* 238). Moreover, 'I do not know' (*BN* 17) also
resounds with the echo of a bell, and that St Mary's bell –

> 'I do not know
> Says the great bell of Bow.'*

We shall appreciate, when we have read *The Dry Salvages*,
that the echo of an incarnational and annunciatory bell is
here especially appropriate.

Other echoes

We enter the garden in pursuit of other echoes. Eliot is an
exact writer. The apparent imprecision here (in relation to

* The echo will not astonish those who have understood that in
Ash Wednesday the poet listened to the same annunciatory bell of St
Mary le bow (*Ash Wednesday* I concludes with recited phrases from the
responsive *Angelus*). He rejected its call to 'turn again' (*AW* I, 1, and
VI, 1) like Dick Whittington and be fêted in the pantomimic Lord
Mayor's Show ('While jewelled unicorns draw by the gilded hearse',
AW, IV, 21: cf. the processional 'Nobody's funeral', *EC* 111; and
cf. 'the pantomime cat' of *Murder in the Cathedral*, page 44. 'Because
I know,' Eliot wrote emphatically in his previous, argumentative
dialogue with the bell, 'that time is always time' (*AW* I, 16), thus
disputing its 'I do not know' as well as its worldly call to 'turn again'.

echoes, bird, and children) is in fact a very special brand of precision. Eliot catches exactly our uncertainty whether there *is* joy and meaningfulness lurking just out of sight, out of grasp; whether the glimpses we have are fragments of a true or of an illusory revelation; whether that which calls or that which impels is indeed reliable and real. Thus the bird is as yet only a bird, or perhaps a deceptive, mimicking 'thrush'. It is to become a dove and the clear symbol of the Holy Spirit only later, in *Little Gidding*. The actual memory, the childhood game in which we hunted for other children, who were hiding from us, leaving us temporarily shut out from their happiness, merges with the image of lonely, bewildered man invited to 'follow' (the reiteration surely gives the word a faint flavour of the demand made by the gospels), but not sure whether what is hinted at and what is just out of sight, out of hearing, is indeed a real happiness or a mockery. (For the hunt is a treasure-hunt too.)

We do follow, returning to our 'first world'. There we become aware of presences, definite, significant, weighty – yet not directly felt by the senses. They are not seen; they are not heard; they do not impress their tread on the dead leaves; but they evidence themselves indirectly by the fact that we recognize our environment as being alert to them. The bird's call is a song obviously responsive to their own music, the very atmosphere is alive with their watchfulness, and the beauty of the roses is of a kind which observation calls out. (This is an important moment. It gives us the first hint of the rose as a symbol of that opened-out, expectant beauty, offering itself, which is later to be folded in the flame of worship, *LG* 257. Thus the rose is established from the start as a symbol of natural beauty and joy, freely given, inviting to the Way of Affirmation, and testifying to the hidden richness and meaning behind what lies about us.)

Some idea of the complexity of Eliot's allusions in this poem may be gathered from closer examination of the imagery in *BN* 27 and 28. The 'unheard music hidden in the shrubbery' (*BN* 27) recalls the 'word unheard' of *Ash*

Wednesday IV and the 'Word unheard' of *Ash Wednesday* V.
In the earlier poem – the record of Eliot's decisive self-dedication as a poet – the vocation was plainly laid upon
him, and reluctantly accepted, to 'redeem the dream', 'the
unread vision in the higher dream', leaving others to look
after the 'gilded hearse' and its 'jewelled unicorns'. The poet
accepted that the word could not 'resound' here,

> 'Not here, there is not enough silence . . .
> The right time and the right place are not here.'

He accepted that the word would have to remain outwardly

> 'unspoken
> Till the wind shake a thousand whispers from the yew'.

The whispers are about us now, as we begin to understand
Four Quartets. The 'wind' (the Holy Spirit) will shake them
from the trees and shrubbery and hedgerows of the Quartets,
if we have a mind to hear.

The phrase, 'the unseen eyebeam crossed' (*BN* 28) is a
notably packed one. Donne's image in his poem *The Ecstasy*
comes to mind –

> 'Our eye-beams twisted, and did thread
> Our eyes upon one double string.'

The echo of Donne's image is faint, but in *East Coker* when
the poet directs the mind back to this experience in the
garden, he writes

> 'The laughter in the garden, echoed ecstasy' (*EC* 131)

and one can no longer doubt that Eliot intended the allusion
to Donne, with its sexual overtones, at this point. Alongside
the introduction of the echo of sexual ecstasy in this para-disal garden scene there are related echoes of the yet unseen
Fall and its consequences, both at the archetypal and at the
personal level. For the juxtaposition of 'beam' and 'crossed'
carries overtones of the Crucifixion, while the words 'unseen
eyebeam' remind us that fallen man queers the pitch in the

created world by failing to see the beam in his own eye (St Luke, VI, 41–2: *EC* 131–3 underlines all these readings).

In this first world, no longer alone, we become aware of order, design and pattern. Here we have a place, are at home, accepting the presences as guests in our world and accepted by them. Our life assumes a shaped artistic delight-fulness as we and they move into the 'box circle' to the centre of square and circle alike. (Further light will be thrown on the imagery at this point, especially as representing the might-have-been past, by reflections which arise naturally from study of *The Dry Salvages*. See pp. 82–4.) And here, at the centre, the moment of revelation is given to us. It is given to us when we are not actively looking for it, not searching the shrubs or the trees to try to locate the hidden laughter and unseen eyes, but looking quietly, undemand-ingly, down into the drained, dry concrete pool, the most commonplace spot – yet at the heart of the garden. The illumination comes suddenly from behind and above when the sun floods the pool with light as though with water, the water lily rises, and on the glittering 'surface' are reflected the presences till this moment invisible.

In view of correspondences that emerge later, building up a firm theological framework, we are justified in reading into this moment a *fiat lux* (Let there be light!). It is the pri-mal creative moment and indicates the presence of the divine Creator (as uncreated Light and Creator of Light, cf. *BN* 135) in the background of *Burnt Norton* as surely as Christ the Redeemer, the Virgin Mary, and the Holy Spirit are respectively present in the subsequent quartets.*

A cloud covers the sun and the momentary revelation is over. It has constituted an instance of the given joy by which we are from time to time made aware of the mystery and the

---

* Eliot's alteration of 'the heart of light' (*BN* 37, cf. *The Waste Land* 41) in earlier editions to 'heart of light' in later editions is perhaps an obvious metrical improvement, but it does also strengthen the echo-by-reversal of Conrad's *Heart of Darkness* (cf. his motto to *The Hollow Men*).

meaning lying behind the temporal order. Such instances, in which the frame of finitude is punctured, are represented here in an experience of natural beauty, but it has a comprehensiveness richer than, say, that of the Wordsworthian mystical moment, for garden and rose carry rich symbolic associations, and anyway we are not alone on a mountain-top but surrounded by the social excitement of laughing, playing children. Moreover we have glimpsed the reflection of unidentified presences with whom the world of *Four Quartets* is gradually to be peopled. And the way in which Eliot peoples the poem may be explored by following the echo 'quietly, quietly' (*BN* 36) to Browning's *Andrea del Sarto*. Andrea invites his wife Lucrezia to sit at his side

'Quietly, quietly, the evening through'

and look through the window at the city of Florence. That a reflection of Dante's city, the *Urbs Beata*, Joyce's 'womancity', the Bride prepared for her Royal Spouse, might be faintly glimpsed through the looking-glass of the pool the reader may yet have to be convinced, but the presence of the painter who mused so long on the might-have-been and daydreamed of the New Jerusalem will be detected by those who have acquired the ear for Eliot's 'unheard music'. Grover Smith* is surely right in discerning Milton's Adam and Eve among the presences 'dignified, invisible' (*BN* 23), and it may well follow (from what is to emerge in later movements – cf. especially *BN* 158 and our comment on it) that the pool is Eve's lake too, in which she saw the fairest of her daughters (cf. *Paradise Lost* V, 462–3, 'I started back/It started back' and *LG* 241).

We need not tease our brains too much with allusions at this stage. The experience in the garden clearly represents the first way of release from the limitations of the temporal: it is the Way of Affirmation, of given joy, unsought illumination. There is so much later in *Four Quartets* of the Way of Negation that it is easy to misunderstand or misrepresent

* Grover Smith, *T. S. Eliot's Poetry and Plays* (p. 260).

Eliot's thinking. It is not all austerity and discipline: it is certainly not life-denying. The *Quartets* begin with a movement in which the rich sacramental depth of life's given delight is asserted as the starting-point in our search for meaning. The moment of illumination is no less real or rich for its brevity. The bird voice which called us, urged us to be quick, and brought us to the spot, now directs us away, for man cannot endure 'much reality', whether of joy, as here, or of suffering (see *BN* 79–81). The 'Go' ('Go ye into all the world') is perhaps as biblical as the 'follow' ('Follow Me') in its religious and moral overtones. It is sound advice to the reader too. It is better to 'go' on than to linger puzzling here over an experience whose meaning is to be gradually filled out for us in backward glances later on.

We must, however, carry forward with us in our reading the parallel firmly established in *BN* 15–17 between the living experience of the garden and the literary experience of reading the poem. Like the garden, the poem is alive with echoes, elusive and tantalizing. If we follow them, perhaps unexpectedly the meaning of the poem will be shown to us at moments of illumination and revelation. Eliot's later practice in this poem will justify us in understanding that the 'leaves' (*BN* 40) of his book, as well as of the garden, are

> 'full of children
> Hidden excitedly, containing laughter' (*BN* 40–1).

II

Garlic and sapphires in the mud

The relationship between time and eternity is a dominant theme in the poem. A momentary experience in which the barrier between the two is breached has been explored in the first movement. As the poem proceeds, further relationships, corresponding to that between time and eternity, are explored both abstractly and concretely – notably the relationships between movement and stillness, change and fixity, flux and pattern. A fit summary of what the poem is about might be to say that it explores moments and modes of reconciliation between these seeming contraries.

In rejecting the straight-line view of time (and consequently the popular current notion of progress, *DS* 87), Eliot appropriately rejects the straight-line course of steadily advancing logic in the poem. As meaning is to be found in life through attention to the moments which puncture the progressive temporal career, so the meaning of the poem is to be found in a series of scattered moments (revelations and images) which, gathered together, eventually reveal the pattern. One can explain this poem at any point only by reference to what is to follow as well as to what has already been said. The throw-back of meaning upon previously half-understood moments ('We had the experience but missed the meaning', *DS* 93) is a feature of life and of *Four Quartets*. We can realize the packed images in the first section of this movement only in terms of later allusions and correspondences. Some of these we must necessarily anticipate.

The images here exemplify the reconciliation between contraries already listed, especially between movement and stillness, and hint at other paradoxes too. The 'bedded axletree' is the pivot of the poem's revolving universe. It is the Cross, the axle on which the temporal-historical revolves, on which the eternal hangs bedded in the soil of earth. (*Our* crucifixion too is that we are bedded in the same soil – shall be bedded even more surely when death comes, *BN* 127.) Garlic and sapphires, the rank plant and the precious stones, may be said to symbolize the paradoxically combined crudity and charm, earthiness and sparkle, of the human flesh in which the tree of life is temporally grounded. Likewise, garlic and sapphires, the plant and mineral which preserve the seeming fixity of the axle-tree, are themselves representative of the superficially still which is hiddenly alive with movement. For the sap courses through the stem of the garlic as it does up the trunk of the tree (*BN* 55) and the compact solidity of the sapphires is built on a tense history of patterned movement at the molecular level. The scar, representing the wound healed and the war forgotten (and therefore linked both with the probing surgeon's work on suffering man, *EC* 149, and with the crust of national harmony now covering old bitter conflicts such as that between Royalist and Cromwellian, *LG* 188) covers the veins of coursing blood at a point where they are in fact most sensitive. The stillness again veils a hidden movement that is live and tense. (We are inevitably reminded by 'trilling wire', *BN* 49, of the stillness of the violin note, *BN* 144. See also *EC* 163, 'The fever sings in mental wires'.)

The rhythmic coursing of blood and sap through human veins and growing trees is part of that dynamic flow sustaining life, however still outwardly. So too the ordered 'drift of stars' is an appearance covering a vitally active reality. As this section concludes 'we' are perhaps lying back on the ground staring up at the 'moving tree' (though this movement might be said to be illusory, the tree being still, the clouds above moving) at a scene whose tranquillity is alive with the delicate patterned shifting of light and shade on flickering leaves. So too, beneath us, on the so solid ground, sodden and still, is the thud of movement, as of boarhound chasing boar. Thus, this way and that, above and beneath, we have seen traced the reconciliation of movement and stillness, flux and pattern.

The image of the axle-tree occurs in Sir John Davies's poem, *Orchestra*, a poem which is important because it has left its imprint on the thought and vocabulary of the *Quartets* at several points. The poem describes the cosmic dance of the created order.

> 'Dancing, bright Lady! then, began to be
> When the first seeds whereof the world did spring;
> The Fire, Air, Earth and Water did agree
> By Love's persuasion (nature's mighty King)
> To leave their first disordered combating;
> And, in a dance, such Measure to observe,
> As all the world their motion should preserve.'

As the cosmic order is a dance, so the dance is a symbol of order at the social and moral level. Time and Dancing, Measure and Movement, are the twin roots of all order – the children of Love. Non-dancing man would introduce an incongruous disorder into his world. (Cf. the climax of the Dead Master's exhortation to the poet, *LG* 146, 'Where you must move in measure, like a dancer'.) The stars and spheres revolve in perpetual dance around Heaven's 'axle-tree'. By the same principle 'Love dances in your pulses and your veins' (*Orchestra*, stanza 106). Eliot's *Quartets* too have each a special relationship to the four elements, air (*Burnt Norton*), earth (*East Coker*), water (*The Dry Salvages*), and fire (*Little Gidding*). It is worth noting therefore that in 'trilling wire' (*BN* 49), with its additional suggestion of telegraph wires, the 'dance along the artery' (*BN* 52), with its hint of a road-way, the 'circulation of the lymph', with its hint of a coursing waterway, and 'drift of stars', we have in succession a dancing movement of each of the elements in turn, air, earth, water, fire – and occurring in the order in which the *Four Quartets* present them.

The image of the 'figured leaf' is one among a number of Tennysonian echoes which carry overtones from *In Memoriam* (here and *BN* 133–4), *Maud* (*EC* 12, *EC* 49, *LG* 59), *Ulysses* (*DS* 24), and possibly *Enoch Arden* (*EC* 123 and *LG* 94). The full significance of these Tennysonian echoes will emerge later (see pp. 34, 48–9, 78, 85, and especially 144–5). Here we are reminded of a passage in which Tennyson sees death as the beginning of a long sleep (a long 'intervital gloom' comparable to the existence 'between two worlds' of which the compound ghost speaks – *Little Gidding*, 122) in which the spirits of men are like 'folded' flowers (cf. *LG* 257) in a garden at night –

> 'So that still garden of the souls
> In many a figured leaf enrolls
> The total world since life began.'
>
> (*In Memoriam* XLIII)

In view of the later, subtler overtones from *Maud* and of the central thematic importance of the garden theme and the image of the folded flower, this echo is significantly indicative of the packed character of Eliot's imagery and of the interlocking network of thematic correspondences which undergirds it. We must also note here that the 'figured leaf' hints at a printed page, and therefore plays its part, if faintly, in sustaining the continuing implicit parallel between living experience and the experience of reading the poem. (See App. III, 5.)

It is notable that the pursuit of boar by boarhound is a straight-line chase in contradistinction to the 'circulation' of the lymph which links us physically in harmonious relationship with the 'drift of stars' and the patterned dance of the universe. The contrast is important. In the human experience of sharing joyfully and peacefully in the ordered life of the cosmos the symbol of the patterned dance for the moment supersedes that of the thrusting, grasping hunt. The process is to be reversed in the 'disturbance' described in *East Coker* II.

The passage we are here attempting to elucidate is the most difficult in *Four Quartets*. The fact that it describes an experience of order glimpsed and fulfilment tasted naturally makes the reader curious about the precise character of the experience. The difficult lines would perhaps allow of sexual interpretation. The image of the tree might be said to carry phallic overtones. The word 'bedded' (*BN* 48) might be cited as giving a hint for a reading of the imagery in sexual terms. On that basis one might interpret the imagery of coursing blood in terms of the sex act. The reading would presuppose that 'we' are lying on the ground, staring up at leaves and sky, and lay great emphasis on the image of the sap rising in the tree. It would also perhaps corroborate the case for reading a special connection between 'the moment' of *BN* 86 and this passage and for detecting Virgilian echoes here. The case would nevertheless remain the product of unsatisfied curiosity rather than of deduction. For this reason we relegate it to a separate Appendix, where the Virgilian influence is more generally under review (App. I).

Connotations which add another note to a verbal chord or another figure to the verbal counterpoint are however always to be reckoned with in reading Eliot. For instance, we must note how *BN* 52–4 may be read in astrological terms. 'The dance along the artery . . . figured in the drift of stars' will mean then that a man's life-span is diagrammatically worked out ('figured') in his horoscope. We may also, in view of the use of the phrase 'floor/Below' (*BN* 58–9), have to reckon with the fact that 'Ascend to summer' (*BN* 55) could call up the connotation of 'summer' as 'a main beam in a structure', 'a horizontal bearing beam in a building' or 'the main beam supporting the girders or joists of a floor . . . or roof' (*O.E.D.*), while not forgetting of course that 'to summer' can be a verb ('to spend the summer'). These connotations would strengthen the case made in Appendix II for detecting special allusive reference here to *Hiawatha*. One must add that the possible echoes of Virgil's *Aeneid* and Longfellow's *Hiawatha* which Appendices I and II respectively explore should not necessarily be regarded as representing rival theories. Multiplicity of echoing is throughout characteristic of *Four Quartets*. Indeed Dante's image of the Car of the Church brought to a standstill in *Purgatorio* XXXII may well represent another fragment in the rich variety of reading which lies behind the teasing lines, *BN* 47–8. And the overtones of *BN* 61, 'reconciled among the stars' may include an allusion to the American flag, the Stars and Stripes, for later echoes involve the American Civil War and the subsequent reconciliation in the structure of historic memories which blends with the fabric of private ones.

Thus it is quite possible that we are at grips here with a cluster of compressed images whose implications extend the range of Eliot's reference over the scope of world history, European history, American history, in developmental terms which touch on the geological, the cultural, the religious and the sexual, blending the macrocosmic and the microcosmic. How justifiable such an assumption is the reader will judge for himself when the full pattern of the poem has emerged.

At the still point of the turning world

Eliot now finds the perfect image for defining the reconciliation between movement and stillness in such a way as to stress its centrality in human experience. At the centre of every revolving wheel or sphere, and therefore at the centre of the turning world itself, is a point which does not move, the still pivotal point whose status is such that the vocabulary neither of stillness nor of movement alone can do justice to it, for it requires the use of both. This point, still, yet the heart of the dance, provides the symbolic expression for the mystery already identified in the experience of revelation recorded in Movement I, where a moment in time took us out of time so that, 'neither flesh nor fleshless', we got our first taste of what Eliot, later in the poem, calls 'Incarnation' (DS 215). This mystery exemplifies a present for once filled full. The present moment, fully realized, is just such a central point, not fixed, not lived through as a mere *after* taking us 'from' the past or as a mere *before* taking us 'towards' the future (BN 63), but alive with the gathered past and future. The potential reality of the present in itself, and not as pathway 'from' past or 'towards' future, is a key theme, cancelling out those notions of inevitable 'ascent' or 'decline'* which colour our thinking when we view our progress through time as a straightforward course (on which things are getting better or worse).

This fully-lived present is rarely tasted. When it is tasted, as it was in Movement I, it leaves us incapable of defining or locating it. We know that it is the pivotal point of stillness which makes movement possible, that it is the centre around which the dance of ordered, significant life takes place, and without which therefore meaningful life would be impossible. We know that we have been there, at that point, in our

* For further thoughts on these two words see page 24.

moments of revelation, but we cannot describe our experience by the familiar vocabulary which places things either temporally or locally; for our experience at the point was precisely an experience of escape from both temporality and locality.

The characteristics of the moment of revelation are now more fully described in moral, physical, and emotional terms. The unity of Eliot's thinking and believing and acting (as a poet) is such that one cannot exclude his philosophy, his moral convictions, or his faith (and even religious practice) from consideration when exploring his poetry. It is not that he allows his personal beliefs to obtrude in the sense that he turns from practising to preaching, from recording experience to moralizing; to put the case like that would be completely to misunderstand Eliot the man and the poet. Rather the case is that his experience, artistry, ideas, and beliefs are so integrated, so firmly and surely inter-related in an astonishingly harmonious pattern of thought, commitment, and action, that any attempt to departmentalize aspects of his life and output for separate treatment would do injury to a richly ordered fabric. Indeed one of the reasons why Eliot's personal convictions do not irritate readers of his poetry to whom those convictions are in themselves alien and even repellent, is that they are so finely harmonized with all that the poet feels and says that they assume an artistic inevitability. They cannot obtrude, because they are not dragged in. They would be awkwardly noticeable, one feels, only if they were left out.

Hence we can comfortably receive from Eliot here a reading of the character of moments of revelation which begins to clarify the fundamental moral and religious position on which the *Quartets* are based. The escape from the temporal is an escape from servitude to 'the practical desire', that desire which keeps us for ever grasping at the future, wanting to *do* something. It is an escape from 'action and suffering', as defined in *Murder in the Cathedral*, from the need to determine events and from subjection to their determining effects, in other words from the compulsion stemming from our own wills and the compulsion exercised upon us from without. Physically this moral freedom is equated with the kind of white light whose very intensity combines steadiness with dazzle. The phrase 'grace of sense' blends the spiritual and the physical, the notions of the divinely given and the humanly assimilable, in the now familiar conjoint balance which gave us 'neither flesh nor fleshless'. Indeed we are still groping towards that full balance of contraries which culminatingly issues in the word 'Incarnation' (*DS* 215). We are uplifted without being shifted, and we taste a concentration of experience which is achieved without any corresponding loss or diminution. To put it crudely, we manage to have it both ways. Seen in the illumination of the revealing moment, the world is new, not by virtue of superseding the old familiar one, but by virtue of making the familiar one clear and meaningful. It becomes at last significant because we cease for a moment to go on 'living and partly living'. The 'partial ecstasy' is fully realized: the 'partial horror' is resolved. That elusive hint of a mystery and a meaning, rich and joyful, just around the corner, just behind the wall, is turned into a realization of their reality; while that ever-intruding hint of a horror and an emptiness just around the corner, just behind the wall, is for once dissolved. The whole Eliot canon has been littered with these hints. The moments of their respective fulfilment and elimination are obviously crucial to the pattern both of his life and of his work.

Eliot has so much to say elsewhere in this poem about the need to escape what he here calls 'the enchainment of past and future' (*BN* 79) that it is important not to underestimate the emphasis he now lays on the positive aspect of the enchainment. Eliot is not a platonist: no Christian ever is. Though man rightly kicks against the fetters of finitude and seeks release from servitude to time, he accepts that the limitations of his situation are protective ones. Fallacious and misleading as the picture of a straight-line progress through time may be, when considered as an attempt to arrive at the *meaning* of existence, that picture is nevertheless directly related to man's natural physical course as a flesh-and-blood creature moving through growth and maturity to decay and death. At the natural physical level we are indeed enchained to the time-sequence in our steady movement from womb to grave. This physical limitation, which prevents us from lingering at the still point of mystical illumination, likewise saves us from all participation in the horror and emptiness whose threat overhangs us at moments of sudden insecurity and lostness. As creatures of flesh and blood, we are not able to endure either the sustained joy or the unbroken vacuity which full release from the temporal would commit us to.

Before leaving this section we should note that here again there are perhaps faint sexual overtones recognizable by those familiar with Eliot's work as a whole. Certainly the words

> 'Neither movement from nor towards,
> Neither ascent nor decline' (*BN* 65–6)

can bear sexual implications if the pun (Neither *assent* nor decline, saying neither yes nor no) is allowed for. Eliot's preoccupation with the feminine conjoint Yes and No, as a sexual equivalent of the human soul's ambiguous response to God's invading demand, is evident in the Choruses of the Women of Canterbury in *Murder in the Cathedral* (cf. p. 90). The significance of the gathered sexual overtones in *Four Quartets* will be noted later. (See pp. 175–7.)

Time past and time future

The positive aspect of our containment by time is put before us again. The time sequence of our natural life may allow for few of those moments in which we are truly conscious, the present being fully realized and the still point reached, but we must not underrate that condition of containment by time which sustains our habitual partial consciousness. Indeed, the positive moments which give us a taste of full consciousness by lifting us out of time are themselves part of the temporal sequence. Only through time can time be transcended. The delights of release and revelation are rooted in simple temporal experiences like that in the rose garden. (And we recall that the poet was looking down un-expectingly and undemandingly when the grace came. He was not eagerly seeking a release, not searching for the hidden voices and presences with the purposefulness of 'practical desire'.) Two other moments of revelation are recalled, each of them private yet also (if Eliot has played the game with us fairly as writer with reader) universal, and realizable as such by dint of thoughtful reading of the poem as a whole. We give reasons in Appendix I for conjecturing that the 'moment in the arbour' (*BN* 86) might refer to the experience of delight also alluded to in the first section of Movement II, an experience whose significance could be guessed if it were allowed that Eliot's record of it carries overtones of Aeneas's love for Dido. We must add that a case might be made for a reference here also to the archetypal incident which is the basis of Eliot's poem *Dans le Restaurant* (and therefore of *Death by Water* in *The Waste Land*). Such multiplicity of reference would be fully explicable and con-gruous. Aeneas's relationship with Dido certainly consti-tutes a *fall* (see pp. 50 and 168) as well as a revelation of delight. A more tenuous conjecture about a possible refer-ence in this line to *Hiawatha* is considered in Appendix II.* These readings remain highly conjectural, but there is firmer ground for reading a multiplicity of reference into 'the moment in the draughty church at smokefall'. It points forward to the experience of the poet as fire-warden, stand-ing in a burnt-out church after a wartime air-raid (*LG* 74–6). But the word 'draughty' (unless it is comically far-fetched) suggests an indoor scene too; so it may well be that the 'draughty church at smokefall' is also the church in the middle of the Eucharist when incense clouds the altar. That

* It should be noted that the validity of other allusions to *Hiawatha* is independent of the possible connection suggested here.

the present is at such times 'involved' (*BN* 88) with past and future is additionally suggestive (since the word stands in close proximity with the image of 'smokefall') for the Latinist who is familiar with Virgil's use of the verb *involvere*. The liturgy gathers together the prayers of living and dead; the eternal intersects the temporal at the point of Consecration. (See pp. 92–3. And for further light on the significance of the three 'moments', *BN* 85–7, see pp. 135–6.)

III

Here is a place of disaffection

Having explored the first way of release from time's bondage, the Way of Affirmation, Eliot is now about to consider the second way, the Way of Negation. As the image of light is the natural image for the poet in his record of an experience of joyful revelation, so the image of darkness will be a needful image in his record of what the way of discipline involves. Before using this image Eliot gives us a picture of the pseudo-darkness which is as different from the fruitful darkness of discipline as the pseudo-light is from the true light, the 'grace of sense', known in the moment out of time. Our own lives are passed largely in the pseudo-light and the pseudo-darkness of living and partly living, in the half-light and half-darkness characteristic of the civilization into which we are born.

The image into which Eliot compresses his critical vision of contemporary civilization is that of the London tube. Here is a 'passage' (cf. *BN* 12) which leads neither into the rose-garden of innocence and revelation nor down to the depths of true mystical self-conquest. Indeed, though it takes us under the earth, it certainly will not lead us to the still centre. It is a place of inner unrest and discontent, so that one does not speak decisively of a time past or a time future, still less of a time present which might livingly involve them both. The poet speaks only of 'time before and time after', and the phrase defies the reader to detect a point of repose. The present is missing altogether from contemporary life, which is spent *en route*. One is always proceeding 'from' or 'towards', in contrast to the stability and centrality of that still centre where there is 'neither from nor towards' (*BN* 63).

Thus the light in the tube is dim, lacking the clarity of daylight, which gives precision and steadiness to what it picks out. For this is a characteristic of sunlight, that its steadiness creates a world of moving shadows such that a reconciliation is effected between stillness and motion, change and permanence. Likewise the dim light in the tube lacks the potency of true darkness, which purges the soul by removing what appeals to the senses and thus directing 'affection' away from what is contained within time to what lies deeper. In short here is neither the nourishment of what truly illuminates nor the cleansing force of that darkness which draws off desire.

In the picture of the passengers each image seems to carry a double weight. Each contributes to the compact pictorial critique of modern life while at the same time tying the passage firmly, backwards and forwards, to what has gone before and to what is to follow. The total network of linked images, symbols and semi-symbols, constitutes a fundamental part of the structure of the *Quartets* as of their meaning. Thus there is neither light nor darkness on the passengers' faces; nor is there that fruitful alternation of the two which effects reconciliation and at least *suggests* 'permanence' (*BN* 95). Instead there is 'only a flicker' revealing faces that are strained by the tyranny of time. The meaningless serial negativity of distraction 'from distraction by distraction', which can lead nowhere, is in sharp contrast with the sure release of a revealing moment or the sure purgation of a cleansing one. The faces that might have been empty of fancies but full of meaning are instead 'filled with fancies and empty of meaning'. The topsy-turvydom extends farther; for the expressions speak not of true fullness ('plenitude', *BN* 99), but of bogus inflation covering nothing ('tumid apathy', *BN* 103). Where the positive moment gave us 'concentration without elimination' (*BN* 75), this picture shows 'no concentration': and the word is a rich one indeed in this poem, carrying as it does the added notion of geometrical concentricity. We are in the inner circle which has no centre. Human beings seem as insignificant as the bits of paper which, like them, are sucked in and out of this false inner world by the mechanical breathing of the ventilation system. They are 'whirled' around in slavery to the machinery. ('Whirled' gives us a cunning pre-echo of lines 113–16, where the word 'world' occurs five times. The pun is Sir John Davies's.* See *Orchestra*, stanza 34 –

> 'Behold the world, how it is whirled round!
> And for it is so whirled, is named so.')

This reading does not of course exhaust the imagery. There is multiplicity of reference here again. Hence one may read the city of London as a whole, rather than merely the underground, into the image of the breathing body. Then the wind 'that blows before and after time' is the daily in and out which gives us the morning and evening rush-hours. Thus 'time' acquires the additional idiomatic connotation of *daily working hours*, particularly appropriate as representing man's slavery to time in the modern mechanized world. Time too is mechanized in this usage. The daily breathing in and out of London's unhealthy lungs sucks men and women in before 'time', and after 'time' (i.e. work), exhales them by 'eructation' into the suburbs. They are borne along by the weary unhealthy breath which sweeps the gloomy hills of this less-than-eternal city. There is no true darkness in this 'twittering world' (another echo from the Virgilian underworld†), where the meaningless, incessant bird-like chatter

* Eliot has used it before in *Ash Wednesday* V –

'Against the World the unstilled world still whirled'.

† See page 154 for further consideration of Virgilian echoes and their significance.

(distracting us from distraction) contrasts so sharply with the articulate call of the guiding bird to follow and 'find' and then to 'go', in Movement I. (The bird spoke humanly there as the human beings twitter bestially here.) These calls gave us an entry into the garden of meaning and an enriched exit, both of them in violent antithesis to the daily entry and exit of London's workers, who come and go to so little purpose.

Before leaving this section we may note that the image of the 'bits of paper' (*BN* 104) eventually links itself with that of the 'dead leaves' (*LG* 83) and, indirectly, with the scattered Sibylline leaves among which we found the fragmented history of the 'Unreal city' in *The Waste Land*. By contrast, the folded leaves of the rose (*LG* 257), and the ordered 'foliage' in the garden, which holds the hidden laughter of children (*BN* 172), are linked with the folded 'figured' leaves of *Four Quartets* (the living poem and the living flower, that restores to life the contents of the 'bowl of rose-leaves', *BN* 16, which is your memory). It is with Dante's symbol of the heavenly rose that the poem finally folds together all that it has reconciled. The thematic order and complexity of the leaves-and-pages imagery are notable.

Descend, lower, descend only

The poet now describes the second way of release from the servitude to time, the Way of Negation. This way leads through the darkness, but it is a deeper darkness than that experienced in the twilight world of the underground. We must go down into the darkness of perpetual solitude. (Here we have an anticipation of the careful distinction made later between the three conditions, attachment, detachment, and indifference, *LG* 150. See pp. 158–9. The world of the London tube, of the daily, mechanically inhaling and exhaling city, is, of course, the sphere of indifference.) We must go down into the world 'which is not world', the world of unworldliness, the world of detachment from all that 'the world' (in the pejorative biblical sense) stands for. (Notice how lines 115–16 – '*Into the world . . . World not world*', but that

which is *not world*' contain unmistakable echoes of St John,
I, 9–10. 'That was the true Light, which lighteth every man
that cometh *into the world*. He was in the *world*, and the *world*
was made by him, and the *world* knew him *not*.' The passage
would be recited regularly in Eliot's hearing as part of the
Last Gospel after the Eucharist. The same passage is echoed
again in *BN* 135–6.) Thus we must strip ourselves of active
delight in that which is to be seen or possessed, relished by
the senses or cherished by the imagination. This disciplined
negating of our possessiveness, drying up of our appetites,
and draining off of our dreams, is to culminate in an 'in-
operacy of the world of spirit'. That is to say that our
austerities are not just selective puritanical rejections of what
outwardly or inwardly appeals to us – for such rejections
might minister only to a greater pride of egotistic spiritual
achievement. (We learned something of this danger from
Murder in the Cathedral.) Rather they must be matched by a
surrender of spiritual claims that is total. We shall be as
undemanding and unexpecting at the climax of these nega-
tions as we were when we looked down, unself-consciously
contemplative, into the drained concrete pool. (And note
that the pool was empty, dry, and drained then, as we are
empty, dry, and drained now – 'Desiccation ... Evacua-
tion ...'.)

This, then, is the Way of Negation, balancing the Way of
Affirmation. (We have shown implicitly that the two ways
not only complement but include each other.) By both
routes we arrive at a stillness, an 'abstention from movement', which represents, spiritually a state of self-surrender,
and morally a condition of no longer desiring those worldly
things that satisfy mind and senses. We take ourselves off the
track on which the worldly move forward through time,
always grasping at what the future is assumed to offer. The
compulsive servitude of the modern world's over-developed
awareness of progress in a straight-line course from past to
future is finely expressed in the image of the 'metalled ways',
with its double hint of packed high-speed roadway (no

'dance along the artery' here: see *BN* 52), and steel railway lines on which one is not even free to steer. The implicit correspondence between attachment to the doctrine of progress and the personal moral habit of living for the future as a slave to practical desire, the intellectual and moral aspects of servitude to time, has been neglected. It represents one of Eliot's most crucial insights.

IV

Time and the bell have buried the day

This beautiful lyric, whose unexpectedness and air of clarity-in-mystery are apt to make one feel that it would be sacrilegious to try to analyse it, nevertheless turns out, as one reflects upon it, to have a very distinct part in the systematic shaping of the poem's total meaning. Eliot has already stressed the given-ness of the moment of revelation in the Way of Affirmation and the arduous, chosen disciplines necessary for seeking release by the Way of Negation. The way of light is a given way: the way of darkness is a chosen way. But Eliot's exploration of this mystery would be incomplete did he not point out that the day of revelation, like every other day, ends in the darkness of night and every lifetime ends in death, so that each man goes by the way of darkness and Negation whether he wants to or not. In death, release by the way of darkness is for once given, and given as unexpectedly as the moment of illumination in Movement I. Hence the appropriate unexpectedness of this lyric. We shall return, if not to the garden, certainly to the soil.

Time will run out and the death-bell will be tolled for each one of us. The cloud will take away earthly sunlight for the last time. The mysteriousness of death and the ambivalence of our attitude to it are reflected in the use here of questions instead of statements. The questions evoke the appropriate doubt about our status after the event, and in particular whether as buried corpses we can be significant any longer in relation to the growing things of earth, the flowers blooming over our heads and the tree roots groping towards us.

Simple paraphrase can do scant justice to the metaphorical harmonics and symbolic overtones. The word 'Time' (*BN* 127) is already charged with special allusiveness from the first three movements of the poem – and indeed from elsewhere in the Eliot canon. Time philosophical and time chronological of Movement I, time mechanical and 'time' industrial of Movement III, will finally tick off the daylight, and the waste land's landlord call 'Time!' for the last time. The word 'bell' is richly loaded to the same extent from images to follow in *The Dry Salvages*. Once one has read the poem as a whole, it is impossible to receive this line (*BN* 127) without echoes from the fog bell at sea and the ground swell (*DS* 34–7), from the annunciations of the Angelus bell and the sanctuary bell. All these will ring away the day for the last time: and the Dayspring will be buried whose death the nightfall shrouded. This point emerges from what follows; for the pun-laden line,

'The black cloud carries the sun (Son) away',

is one of the most packed lines in the poem. To begin with, cloud carries the sun away in each of the three moments (and their three 'falls') listed in *BN* 85–7. The 'moment in the rose-garden' ends with the line,

'Then a cloud passed, and the pool was empty' (*BN* 39).

As 'smokefall' hides the sanctuary at the moment of consecration and sacrifice (marked by bells), so there was darkness over all the land at the Crucifixion, and a cloud carried away the Son at the Ascension. (These correspondences depend on readings yet to be encountered. We do not pretend that they emerge clearly from the text up to this point. For fuller consideration of the theme, see p. 135.) The clutching and clinging of tendril and spray, in the context, cannot but remind us that the axle-tree Cross is bedded in the clotted mud (*BN* 47–8) as the crucified son of man is buried in the soil.

Chill

No word could have more surely illustrated the richness of reference which we are here recording than this word 'chill'. For it is given a paramount emphasis here and it is used only once more in the poem – in connection with the purgatorial suffering of the human 'patient' who has put himself into the bleeding hands of the suffering surgeon, Christ. (See *EC* 162, 'The chill ascends from feet to knees'.) For anyone deeply read in the poem, the image of chill fingers curling down, brought into inevitable relationship with that of the patient who lies probed by the surgeon's steel (*EC* 147 ff.), hints at correspondences full of paradox and mystery.

After the questions, something like an answer is given us in the last three lines of the lyric. The known light will have gone out for us, the bird's wing having thrown back for the last time in our sight a flicker of reflected sunlight (and sunlight reflected was all that we were able to endure in our moments of delight in the earthly rose-garden), but 'the light is still' (that is, both 'steady' and 'continuingly') at the centre of the world – and true light, not reflected light this time. Since we are, physically speaking, ourselves a little nearer to this centre, the lyric ends with a gleam of hope, as of light, even on the most superficial reading. But there is more to be said than that. The comforting bird who has, during our lifetime, thrown before our eyes fitful reflected glimpses of the sun's light, is here a 'kingfisher'. 'Fisher' (of men) carries apostolic overtones, and the Fisher king, to the reader of *The Waste Land* and Jessie Weston's *From Ritual to Romance* is a symbol of divine Sovereignty suffering for the wasted kingdom. There is probably, therefore, reference to the Church in the image of 'the kingfisher's wing'. Some such correspondence seems to be implicit in lines 134–6

'After the kingfisher's wing
 Has answered light to light, and is silent, the light is still
 At the still point of the turning world.'

These lines echo St John, I, 8–9,

> 'The same came for a witness, to bear witness of the Light, that all men through him might believe. He was not that Light, but was sent to bear witness of that Light. That was the true Light, which lighteth every man that cometh into the world.'

This is part of the Last Gospel, already echoed in *BN* 115–16. The Last Gospel, of course, comes after the end of the Eucharist. This is not the only liturgical echo, however. For 'light to light' (*BN* 135) subtly echoes conjointly 'Light of Light' (from the Creed) and 'dust to dust' (from the Burial Service) in what is an instance of Joycean compression. (This sudden 'shaft of sunlight' shows up the dust because of the relationship between light and dust established by Eliot's verbal counterpoint. Cf. *BN* 169–70 and *LG* 56–7.) These correspondences make clear one of the connotations of the words 'answered' and 'silent' used here as of 'light'. The Church (the priest) has spoken the last words of the Mass, has said the last prayers of committal over the dying man and over the dead man. One more human life is over. One more re-enactment of the ever-recurring divine sacrifice has been worked through within the sphere of incarnation.

It is difficult to know where to draw the line in tracing the sources of literary echoes, but in view of correspondences elsewhere in the poem (see pp. 49 and 85), it should be noted that the image of the yew (*BN* 133) brings a clear recollection of Tennyson's *In Memoriam*.

> 'Old Yew, which graspest at the stones
> That name the underlying dead,
> Thy fibres net the dreamless head,
> Thy roots are wrapt about the bones.'
>
> (I.M. Section II)

> 'Old Warder of these buried bones,
> And answering now my random stroke
> With fruitful cloud and living smoke,
> Dark yew, that graspest at the stones
> And dippest toward the dreamless head. . . .'
>
> (I.M. Section XXXIX)

It should also be noted that *BN* 135–6,

> 'the light is still
> At the still point of the turning world',

so closely echoes *Ash Wednesday* V

> 'And the light shone in darkness and
> Against the World the unstilled world still whirled
> About the centre of the silent Word.'

as to establish a firm link between 'light' and 'Word' in the Eliot canon. The link corroborates our reading of 'light' as calling up in this quartet the image, Light of light. Although this lyric is concerned with death, its conclusion makes it an affirmative utterance. For after each withdrawal of light or Light, whether at the end of a moment of revelation, at the end of a day or a lifetime, whether at the coming of darkness after the Crucifixion or the coming of the cloud at the Ascension, the unreflected, uncreated Light still remains at the centre of the living cycle of our experience. The circumference of earth and time and experience moves through alternate light and darkness (cf. *BN* 95 – 'With slow rotation suggesting permanence'), but the uncreated Light, God the Creator is 'still' (in every sense of the word) unchangingly at the centre. It is His presence that conclusively dominates this lyric and gives a corresponding character to *Burnt Norton* as a whole.

V

Words move, music moves

Eliot insists throughout this poem that meaning cannot be derived from the flow of time, but only from intermittent moments of illumination abstracted from that flow and woven into a pattern. Here he finds a fruitful series of images to give concrete expression to this notion. Indeed the images together constitute an analogy which grows into something more than a mere analogy – rather a further citation of the same truth. The analogy is provided by the work of art – and by poetic utterance especially.

Words and music move only in time. A poem or a symphony may be printed on paper, but they can be actually performed only through a given sequence of minutes. Speech breaks out of silence and, when finished, ends in silence. A piece of music is the same. Neither words nor notes can achieve the permanence which guarantees survival, unless they are shaped into a pattern as a poem, a play, or a symphony. It is the pattern, the form, that makes exact repetition in performance possible, and thereby gives to verbal and musical utterance the stability ('the stillness' – the capacity to be always there) which a work of art like a Chinese jar has. Thus in many ways art provides examples of how movement and stillness can be reconciled and stability moulded out of the flux of time. Poetry and music move 'in time' both in the sense that they have metrical measure and in the sense that in performance they begin and end. But the pattern gives them stillness in spite of the fact that movement is of their essence. Conversely, the live outlines of a Chinese jar give it unceasing 'movement' in spite of the fact that stillness is of its essence.

Eliot is at pains to distinguish clearly the character of stillness and stability which pattern imposes on a work of art (because it provides such an excellent analogy of what the relationship of the temporal to the eternal must be). It is not just that the throbbing violin string and moving sound waves produce a still note – for of course that note is itself extended in time. Rather it is that the pattern of a musical movement is such that beginning, middle, and end, exist contemporaneously. The first bar of the symphonic movement would be strictly meaningless were it not that the last bar already exists and indeed (to speak in terms of form) is already present to the mind of the intelligent listener. Just so the middle bars of the movement take their meaning from what is to follow and make sense by the fact that beginning

and end are present with them. The coexistence of beginning, middle, and end, which is what the pattern has
established, gives meaning and permanence to the symphony
or the poem. For it is plain that the first line of a poem is as
meaningless without what follows it as the first bar of a
symphony would be.

Eliot presses this analogy firmly upon us in a series of
apparent paradoxes. The end of the symphony 'precedes the
beginning' (*BN* 146) in that it is present to the minds of
conductor, players, and audience alike (those of them who
know the work) before performance begins. End and
beginning both together coexist in the very fact of the
symphony, before the performance begins and after the performance ends. The whole is always 'present' now, for the
pattern has virtually eternalised this thing which yet moves
only 'in time', can only live and die in each successive performance.

The grappling with this notion produces in the poet's
mind an acute awareness of the obduracy of words – their
resistance to attempts to make them say what one wants them
to say. (On *BN* 151 see also Appendix III, 1.) Thus Eliot has
something to say about his own professional task in the making of poetry. What he has to say is not dragged in. It is of
the poem's essence, so that once more we are conscious of
the remarkable unity of Eliot's thought and life and work, a
unity which harmonizes faith and scholarship, practice and
poetic craftsmanship, into a single pattern. Moreover, we
must note that in a poem in which Eliot has already addressed the reader in *his* present capacity (as a man reading a
poem, listening to the voice of a poet, *BN* 14), it is highly
proper that the poet should speak frankly in his own immediate capacity, as a man writing a poem, struggling with
words and trying to knock them into shape. Unless the
generalizations about human life fit every situation, are
indeed relevant to this immediate now, the task at this
moment on hand, they are neither fully apt nor universally
valid. And unless the poet speaks as exactly what he is – a

man writing poetry – to the reader as exactly what *he* is – a man reading poetry, the truth of the living present will not have been touched upon. We shall have been talking about a highly artificial, abstract present – perhaps it would not be too strong to say a false present. Eliot will not evade the ultimate demand of truth that it should not be isolatable from the truth-speaker, should not be something to which the true utterance points, but something of which the true utterance partakes, and indeed something which the true utterance manifests both in its own matter and in its own form. The truth of the *Quartets* is here present in their writing, here in their reading, here in their understanding, in their performance, as it is there present in the matters to which they draw our attention, or rather in the matters in which they involve us. For, strictly speaking, they draw our attention to nothing. Rather they commit us to an experience which is a re-living of experience and an anticipation of experience – and not only ours, but the poet's, and not only his, but humanity's (and 'not the experience of one life only'; see *DS* 98). The poems do not tell us about, but take us into, a present in which past and future are contained, a present filled full of meaning by virtue of the patterned moments of illumination it is capable of bearing.

Eliot's grappling with words, therefore, in the attempt to impose pattern and order, is in perfect correspondence with everyman's encounter with experience, and his desire to impose pattern and order upon it. The words are both too weak to bear the burden of meaning we would put upon them, and too slippery, shifting, and changing, to be organized into exactly articulated formulation. Like human creatures themselves, they are constantly under attack from the diabolical forces of disorder, indiscipline, evil passion, and triviality. Even so the true Word, Christ himself, was tempted in the desert. Here, if anywhere, is the climax of *Burnt Norton*. We have reached the point at which the Word is uttered. And its utterance has issued naturally out of the personal, yet universal, existential situation. Sure form is

given at last to the 'echoes' that filled our moment of revelation in Movement I. We know now why 'echoes' was the
right term for those presences that seemed to be about us in
our first world, for that sensed depth and mystery and
meaningfulness surrounding the joy given in the Way of
Affirmation. But Eliot's is not a preached, scarcely even a
proclaimed, word. It is an uttered Word, grasped at amidst
the slipping and slithering of human words and the baying
and chattering of diabolical voices. It is not the triumphant
Word either: it is the 'Word in the desert'.

The 'voices of temptation' are twofold, those that inter-
rupt the dance of life (which is a continuing funeral dance;
see *EC* 110–11), with the shadow of doubt and fear; and
those which tempt to despair as man recognizes his own sinfulness. This interpretation of the line

> 'The loud lament of the disconsolate chimera'

assumes that the chimera is a lady metamorphosed who has
seen her animal face reflected in water. (A cloud mercifully
covered the sun before we had time to catch sight of our
own faces thrown back by its light from the garden pool.)
The legend is given the same moral and spiritual force by
Sir John Davies in *Nosce Teipsum*.

> 'As in the fable of that Lady fair
> Which for her lust was turned into a cow;
> When thirsty to a stream she did repair,
> And saw herself transformed (she wist not how;)
>
> At first she startles! then, she stands amazed!
> At last, with terror, she from thence doth fly,
> And loathes the wat'ry glass wherein she gazed,
> And shuns it still, though she for thirst do die,
>
> Even so, Man's Soul, which did God's Image bear,
> And was, at first, fair, good, and spotless pure;
> Since with her sins, her beauties blotted were,
> Doth, of all sights, her own sight least endure.

For even, at first reflection, she espies
Such strange CHIMERAS and such monsters there!
Such toys! such antics! and such vanities!
As she retires, and shrinks for shame and fear.

The detail of the pattern is movement

In conclusion the theme of reconciliation is rehearsed again, first abstractly, then concretely. Thus, in St John of the Cross's study of the discipline of contemplation as the way to joy, the symbol of a ladder with ten steps is employed. The stillness of mystical contemplation is the end, but the saint has to use the image of movement up stairs in order to define the means. As in the dance, so even in the mystic's exercises, the detail is movement though the overall end is that which does not change – arrival at a pattern which eternalizes the whole. Human desire, casting the grasp forward and enslaving us to time, has been shown to be 'undesirable', yet its movement is towards that which is unchanging – Love. For the love we seek, changeless, secure, 'unmoving', being the cause of our seeking, is the cause of movement and its 'end' too. Thus, within time, human hunger for that timeless and changeless love can be fed only by limited, partial satisfactions snatched at by creatures who are pinned to a level of half-conscious half-existence by the bonds of finitude.

Hence the shaft of sunlight brought the revelation in the garden. Hence too the poet's words, disturbing the dust from the rose-leaves in the reader's mind (bringing into the light the reader's own personal equivalent of the revelation in the garden) may have brought back echoes of the rich joy hidden all about us, just out of sight. Such moments of revelation form the basis of a meaningful reading of the human situation and justly therefore make the rest of our earthly experience seem trivial, empty, and joyless by comparison.

East Coker

In my beginning is my end. In succession

East Coker in Somerset is the village where a distinguished sixteenth-century member of the Eliot family, Sir Thomas Elyot, lived. Sir Thomas Elyot's treatise on education, *The Governour*, was published in 1531. Eliot's specific allusions to this book in the first movement of this second *Quartet* (27 ff.) and the clear influence of the book at other points give it a special importance for the reader.

Mary Stuart's motto, 'In my end is my beginning', is reversed in the poet's opening sentence. The reversal is in itself an instance of that emphasis upon circularity rather than upon straight-line progress as the basis of meaningful patterning, which the poem as a whole insists upon. You end where you begin: you begin where you end. Eliot restores Mary Stuart's motto to its original order at the end of *East Coker* (*EC* 209), thus completing the circuit. (Like the buildings, the sentence has crumbled and been restored.)

The process which we call 'succession' is not a straight-line process, as it appears to be superficially, but a circular one; for it is cyclic. 'Houses rise and fall.' Buildings crumble and decay; and they may be restored. (There is a cyclic movement from solidity to decay and back to solidity.) Or they are demolished, removed, and replaced by open land, new buildings, or roads. The larger cyclic pattern is traced in the use of stone from demolished buildings to make new buildings, and in the burning of old timber (that is, both beams from demolished buildings and also coal) in new fires, whereby wood from trees grown in the earth makes its way back to earth in the form of ash. And this earth is itself composed of decayed matter from vegetable, animal, and human life. Man is nourished on the 'cornstalk and leaf' which later he nourishes by his own faeces and by the rotting bone of his buried body. Thus whether we consider the progress of material civilization – buildings and the like – or of human life, the cyclic pattern is evident.

It is clear now, if not earlier, that 'Houses rise and fall' (*EC* 2) refers to families and dynasties as well as to buildings. We might have guessed that, since the opening motto directed thought to the House of Stuart. The cycle of birth, growth, decay, and death, evident in man's individual life and family life, and also at the social and civilizational level, binds us to the earth from which we draw our nourishment and to which we return, the earth from which we obtain our stone and wood and to which these materials must return as crumbled masonry, roadway rubble, or burnt ash. (It is significant in relation to the overall network of correspondences which establish the 'meaning' of this poem that stone is destroyed by air or water – hence Eliot's use here of the word 'crumble' – and wood by fire. The work of all the elements is involved in this cyclic pattern. The link here with Sir Thomas Elyot's thinking is notable. See pp. 44 ff.)

The sentence 'Houses live and die' (*EC* 9) directs attention to the flourishing and waning of both families and buildings. Notice how, between the phrase 'time for building' and the lines describing the decayed family house, Eliot interposes 'a time for living and for generation' (*EC* 10), thereby, as it were, *containing* the personal human cycle within the larger pattern of the building's career. The concrete images in which the decaying house is pictured carry overtones of the Elizabethan and the Gothic ('wainscot', 'arras') sufficient to keep in the back of the reader's mind the house of Elyot at East Coker, the House of Stuart, and perhaps, in view of Eliot's interest in Poe, the house of Usher. (The blending of personal and national, Elyot and Stuart, is characteristic of the poet's practice throughout. The 'silent motto', as Elizabeth Drew has pointed out, may refer equally to Mary Stuart's motto and to Eliot's *tace et fac*.)

The reference to the wainscot and the field-mouse (*EC* 12) is to be taken up again in *LG* 59 ('The wall, the wainscot and the mouse'). In view of the echoes which we shall hear later (*EC* 49), it should be noted that the lover in Tennyson's *Maud* speaks of 'the shrieking rush of the wainscot mouse' (*Maud* VI, viii, 9).

In my beginning is my end. Now the light falls

We move appropriately from the general to the particular. It now appears that the poet is actually revisiting the ancestral village and the site of the ancestral home. The way of course is the straight-line way through history which none of us can evade – the road. And it is notable that the 'deep lane' takes on the character of the Underground. It is the rural equivalent of the London Tube, shuttered with trees from the sun's full light, 'dark in the afternoon', and *insisting* on the direction with that compulsiveness which is characteristic in this poem of Eliot's railways and of the appetitive, forward-looking desires with which they are associated. The heat is 'electric', the atmosphere sultry and hypnotic. If the overtones of artificiality and unreality link the scene with the images of the London Tube (*BN* 92 ff., *EC* 118 ff.), the emphasis on the fact that here is a darkness in the afternoon, a taste of night in the middle of the day, when the dahlias sleep, links the scene by contrast with those images in which spring or summer is suddenly tasted in the middle of winter (see *EC* 51 and the opening of *LG*, 'Midwinter spring is its own season'). These moments in which the familiar pattern of the seasons is broken symbolize the revelatory moments of intersection between the timeless and time. The intrusion of spring or summer into winter, of light into darkness, matches the unexpectedly given experience of joyful illumination. The intrusion of winter into summer, of darkness into light, of night into day, matches the personal and archetypal experiences alike of darkness and discipline, of death and negation, of the demand for surrender and the Crucifixion. Hence the way here, 'shuttered with branches', has the light shut off by the sheltering but shadowing trees which carry overtones of the Cross. And the phrase 'dark in the afternoon' reverberates with echoes of the darkness over all the land that followed the death of Christ, as did the line 'The black cloud carries the sun away' (*BN* 128).

In that open field

The dreamlike picture of the past which is conjured up as the poet stares at the open field is firmly framed. The repetition of 'If you do not come too close' (*EC* 24) and the reference to the 'weak pipe' and 'little drum' give the picture a flavour of fairy-tale fantasy. We are not told that the 'open field' is the exact site of the former Elyot family home, but the incantatory repetition ('Is an open field', *EC* 4. 'Across the open field,' *EC* 15, 'In that open field', *EC* 23) puts the field at the centre of our view. The repetition also brings to mind the Open Field system of farming especially associated with medieval manorial estates. The system involved annual rotation of crops over three large fields, often one for wheat (the bread crop), another for barley (the drink crop), and the third lying fallow. The cyclic orderliness of this rotation in the background has a peculiar appropriateness in the present context. This is the place in space where Sir Thomas Elyot's account of human dancing comes back to life. The phrases exactly echo Sir Thomas's own (see *The Governour*, Bk I, xxi). The archaic spelling is reproduced. And it is important that for Sir Thomas dancing is not just a symbol of marriage and of social harmony: it is a symbol of universal harmony. Sir Thomas's book begins with a standard sixteenth-century account of the hierarchical order governing the universe. It is the preservation of degree which distinguishes creation and order from chaos. The four elements, earth, water, air, and fire, of which the natural order is compounded, must keep their proper places. Man, who is fashioned of the same elements, a microcosm of the whole, must order his life accordingly. At the cosmic, social, and personal levels, the hierarchically ordered dance is the basis of all harmony and

44

the true expression of that Love which must govern all things. We know from Shakespeare's plays how deeply this ancient sense of the meaning of degree had bitten into the pre-modern mind. The intrusion of disorder into nature and life, upsetting the hierarchical health of the cosmos, the body politic, the body domestic, and the microcosmic human hero, is a central issue of Shakespearean tragedy. Thus Eliot's twentieth-century treatment of universal themes on the basis of the four elements (Air – *Burnt Norton*; Earth – *East Coker*; Water – *The Dry Salvages*; and Fire – *Little Gidding*) recapitulates the work of his family and philosophical ancestor, Elyot, as it does that of his poetic ancestors, Shakespeare and Sir Thomas Davies. In this sense the task of poet and teacher is only and always to rediscover what 'has already been discovered/Once or twice, or several times, by men whom one cannot hope/To emulate' (*EC* 183–5); and so even poetic and cultural activity partakes of the cyclic quality of life within time, and cannot therefore be fairly represented in the idiom of 'progressive' thought. Indeed as new houses are made from the *crumbled* houses of the past (see *EC* 2), so Eliot's *Four Quartets* are made from the crumbled poems of the past.

One must not ignore the heavily didactic quality of Elyot's thought, for moral implications are carried over into Eliot's re-minting of it. Thus, in Elyot, the 'concorde' betokened in the dance of man with woman, holding 'eche other by the hand or the arm', is not a vague harmony or good-fellowship. It is a blending of potentialities and a cancelling out of extreme centripetal tendencies, that together guarantee the preservation of 'severity' (as opposed to ferocity on the one hand, mildness on the other), magnanimity, constancy, honour, wisdom, and continence. 'These qualities, in this wise being knitte together, and signified in the personages of man and woman daunsinge, do expresse or sette out the figure of very nobilitie. . . .' (Note that 'figure' is an important word in *Burnt Norton*.) For Elyot the various figures of the dance can each be equated with moral or social virtues ('prudence', 'industry', 'circumspection', 'modesty', and the like). The subject has its bearing on Eliot's philosophical and sociological thinking.

Dancing round the fire (its leaping flames and flying sparks are an essential feature of the elemental cosmic dance for the sixteenth-century mind), joining in circles, blending and balancing solemnity with laughter (the dance of the 'humours' matching the dance of the elements), the long-dead peasants lift earth-laden feet above the earth and plant them back on the earth, thus repeating in miniature the whole cycle of human life. So doing, they *keep time.**
(According to Sir John Davies, Time and Dancing, Measure and Movement, are the twin principles of all order – the children of Love.

> 'Reason hath both their pictures in her Treasure;
> Where Time the Measure of all moving is,
> And Dancing is a moving all in measure . . .' *Orchestra*, st. 23.)

And so doing, they reproduce the rhythm of the cyclic seasons (just as in the 'constellations' the cosmic dance of the stars continues, *BN* 54), the rhythm of nourishing and harvesting, growing and breeding. Feet rise and fall in the dance and in copulation, as in the pattern of life from cradle to grave. The cycle of nourishment is from cornstalk, to eating, to dung. The cycle of life is from coupling on the 'sodden floor' (*BN* 58) to burial under the yew tree (*BN* 133). The patterns close in dung and death.

Dawn points, and another day

It would be contrary to the whole pattern and meaning of the poem to preserve a chronological logic of succession. It would falsify all that is said in the poem of where true meaning is to be found and by what principles pattern can be discerned and order constituted. Hence the sudden changes of time and place. We carry with us into another day the important image of the poet as a concealed observer,

* 'Keeping time', *EC* 39, echoes Poe's *The Bells* of course.

through the night, of music and dancing from which he was excluded, as he was from the hidden music and laughter of the garden. The present into which we were taken when we joined the poet in his walk down the deep lane into the village (*EC* 15 ff.) became itself enriched and rendered meaningful by the taking into it of the poet's own family past, together with the cultural past of the society to which he belongs. But this enrichment remains an enrichment *of the present*. We cannot, must not seek to, return to the past. We stopped and listened momentarily to the pipe and drum, heralding a recall of the past, but we must not 'follow an antique drum' (*LG* 187), for following is another matter – the proper response to 'Other echoes' (*BN* 16). So we are lifted back into the present, established again within the time-scheme where dawn *points* (a defining, focusing, and forward-looking gesture with the compulsiveness of the lane's *insistence* 'on the direction into the village', *EC* 18), to the day which 'in succession' follows its predecessor. This day, by its 'heat and silence' will have that artificial, compulsive, half-lit, character which belongs to the tunnel-like temporal way, as represented in the rural lane as well as in the urban underground.

Out at sea too (over water as well as over land) time flows by. For the 'dawn wind' as it 'wrinkles' the surface of the sea, ages what it touches, and indeed decays itself, for the word 'slides' brings back forcibly the image of the poet's struggle to reduce to order the anarchic, decaying words which 'slip, slide, perish' (*BN* 151). There is an implicit parallel in the notional framework of the poem between the ordered movement of the dance and the ordering of words in speech. The parallel is explicit in Sir John Davies. In human utterance air is *ordered* into speech: speech is dancing air: the utterance of the word disciplines air into a pattern. The image is fruitful of theological and poetic correspondences. As human speech disciplines air into a pattern, so the human frame disciplines earth into a pattern. Thus the fuller realization of the cosmic dance, as the pattern of all order and culture, makes clear why the utterance of the Word, and the ubiquitous reflection of it in echoes, were dominant themes in *Burnt Norton*, the quartet concerned with the element air.

The immediate concern here, however, (*EC* 49–50), is the indecisiveness of the poet's placing. His location is not to be defined by the familiar spatial or temporal criteria. (Only later shall we fully understand why, among possible locations, the poet suddenly speaks as from the coastline. See pp. 82–4. Thus once more in the very construction of the poem the 'future' – *DS* 15 ff. – is gathered into the present, which has just similarly gathered the past into itself.) The poet will not find meaning at the level of 'succession' either as person or as writer. He must plant himself centrally and re-plant himself so. Hence the movement ends in the middle of the motto. 'In my beginning.' Reader and poet together stand poised in the unfinished present where alone the past can be recovered and the pattern discerned.

More needs to be said, however, about the crucial phrase, 'I am here' (*EC* 49). Eliot's technique of using phrases which exploit the line-end by leading the reader to half-expect something which does not follow in the next line, is practised with special sharpness and subtlety in *Four Quartets*. He thereby achieves a fruitful ambiguity, blending in additional overtones of meaning, and incidentally giving the reader a first-hand experience of the might-have-been. (There is a firm instance of this practice in *Little Gidding*, line 42, where the line-end,

'you would have to put off'

leads the reader, in view of the context, to half-expect the biblical

'Put off thy shoes from off thy feet . . .' see p. 132.)

The device is a refinement of the practice of beginning well-known quotations only to break in on them in the middle, when expectancy has been aroused, with new sequences which strongly contrast in tone and mood with the quoted opening. (Cf. what follows on 'When lovely woman stoops to folly and', *Waste Land* 253, or on 'For Thine is the' at the conclusion of *The Hollow Men*.) It will be agreed that the more subtle the use of this device, the less sure will the reader be that the poet consciously intended the effect which he discerns. Nevertheless, increasing familiarity with *Four Quartets* convinces me that the line-end

'I am here' (*EC* 49)

is meant to lead the reader to half-expect

'I am here at the gate alone'

from Tennyson's *Maud*. Echoes of Tennyson's *In Memoriam* (see pp. 18 and 34) and of his *Ulysses* (see pp. 78 and 85) are noted elsewhere. The parallel with *Maud* is, on investigation, a rich one. The lover is waiting at dawn. He has been shut out all night from the music and dancing

'the dancers dancing in tune
Till a silence fell with the waking bird
And a hush with the setting moon.'

Moreover there are strong correspondences between *Burnt Norton* and *Come into the garden, Maud* in the garden imagery and in the visitor's situation. The lily and the rose are dominant and powerful images in *Come into the garden, Maud*. The lover, consciously excluded from the games and revelry which are so near and yet so far (cf. echoes of the return of the Prodigal Son in *Little Gidding*: see pp. 128 and 153), communes at length with lily and rose, and

'long by the garden lake I stood
For I heard your rivulet fall.'

The heard, but unseen, waterfall is part of the garden imagery when the garden is 'recovered' at the end of *Little Gidding*,

'The voice of the hidden waterfall' (*LG* 247).

And in the same passage there is a further reference in the garden imagery to

'unknown, remembered gate' (*LG* 243, cf. *BN* 20)

which perhaps most significantly of all corroborates our reading of a decisive and indeed important echo of *Maud* at this present point. The poet is *at the gate*, and he is *alone*.

II

What is the late November doing

There is much to suggest that the personal emotional history of the poet may be present with especial strength behind the powerful evocative imagery of Movement II (first part) in each of the *Quartets*. It is not necessary to accept the conjecture that the opening of Movement II of *Burnt Norton* recalls Aeneas and Dido (see Appendix I) or even to allow that it refers to a sexual experience, in order to confirm that the passage defines a moment of release into full awareness of reconciliation, full participation in the dance of life; and it is not necessary to pry into the poet's private biography in order to assume the expression of the personal and the particular within the universal. The poet's use of the word 'we' (*BN* 56), reaching out as it does to involve the reader, ensures that blend of universal and particular, epic and private, by which Eliot commits to one statement the experience of poet, reader, and man-in-history (not to mention man-in-Literature).

If the lyrical passage which opens Movement II of *Burnt Norton* takes us back to an experience of joy tasted and cosmic harmony shared (whether or not the experience has the Carthaginian character of an embroiling love from which the young man who is properly 'pius' will be withdrawn by the force of his personal vocation, and whether or not it carries a half-hidden involvement of romantic youthful memories reaching out to *Hiawatha*), then the lyrical passage here, opening Movement II of *East Coker*, seems to point to a re-awakening of delight (perhaps of love) in middle age, which threatens all patterns, seasonal or cyclic, with destruction. This recrudescence of spring in November is not only a revelatory release from time, but also an indication of the imminent possibility of a derangement which can only end in the 'destructive fire'. Thus the imagery here reflects movement in a predominantly converse direction to that in the corresponding lyrical section of *Burnt Norton*. There the orderly dance of life in human veins, growing trees, and drifting stars replaced the thrusting hunt, 'the boarhound and the boar', by a pattern of reconciliation involving man and the earth and the heavens. Here there is no orderly dance in the natural world but a 'disturbance' by which growing things writhe inappropriately (disobediently, one might say, to speak Elizabethanly) under human feet; hollyhocks strive to assert themselves too loftily (proudly, Sir Thomas Elyot might have said); and roses, also over-eager by prolonging their lives to forget their due hierarchical status, pay the price of their presumption and tumble down under the weight of early snow. The derangement at the earthly and vegetable level is figured in a corresponding derangement at the stellar level. The sun or the lightning in the *Burnt Norton* lyric lit up the leaf of the moving tree perhaps above an act of human love by which long-forgotten wars were appeased. Here the thunder of the stars simulates the noise of human warfare as the Sun, in the month of November, finds itself challenged in the house of Scorpio. The Carthaginian love, or whatever it was, appeased human wars. The November disturbance threatens involvement in a cosmic war. Indeed vocabulary and imagery carry overtones not only of the War in Heaven (*EC* 60–1) and of the earth's tortuous pre-history (*EC* 66), but also of national strife as pre-figured, for instance, in the Prophecies of Merlin. (In this connection it is worth comparing *EC* 58 ff. with the conclusion of Chapter iv, Book VIII, of Geoffrey of Monmouth's *Histories of the Kings of Britain*.) Thus associations of national history and conflict are merged with cosmic and personal ones.

Finally sun and moon, flying comets and meteorites, present us with a scene in which the dance has given place to the hunt (as the hunt in *BN* II gave place to the dance) – a hunt of macrocosmic dimensions, sweeping the skies and the 'plains' of the earth alike. The climax is represented by a whirling (see comment on *BN* 104) in which dance-like circulation is distorted into the misshapen revolution of the vortex. The image, with its inevitable associations of irresistible suction, fitly hints at a force capable of dragging the world from its true centre into the range of a 'destructive fire'. How far the challenged Sun and the Sun gone down of lines 61–2 suggest a rebellion against the divine law in terms of Crucifixion will depend on the reader's sensitivities. Certainly these two images, and those of man and nature scorched and tumbled after a presumptuous neglection of degree (to use Shakespeare's apt phrase in *Troilus and Cressida*) might form an apt network of symbols in relation to the Crucifixion. The inevitability of old age, whose glacial character succeeds the autumnal disturbances of middle age, is finely impressed upon us in the 'cap' of 'ice-cap'. Here is another crowning that awaits us (to set a crown upon a 'lifetime's effort', *LG* 130).

That was a way of putting it – not very satisfactory

After contemplating the 'present' of his own personal emotional life in the first section of this movement, the poet again quickly re-plants himself in the 'present' in which the poem is being written. Thus once more the poet achieves the immediacy of the writer-reader relationship. The writer's admission that he wrestles laboriously with words in the never 'very satisfactory' effort to express his meaning establishes a double link of sympathy with the reader. It is not just that the reader enjoys being taken into the poet's confidence; he is also comforted to learn that, if he finds the poem difficult, reading it slow and toilsome, this is not

because a clever poet has intentionally manufactured a test-
ing puzzle for him, but because a struggling human being
like himself has been doing his best to make sense of
experience. Reader and writer are suddenly side by side,
involved in the same 'intolerable wrestle with words and
meanings'.*

The poet, then, looking back on his image-packed attempt
to describe the November disturbance, finds it over-wordy,
outmoded, too consciously poetic. (The lapse into writing
archaically was itself a disturbance of the twentieth-century
cultural present.) Thus the poet reduces the stature of the
passage to that of a poem within the poem. It is of course
fair to admit that one result of Eliot's method here is that
he can both have his cake and eat it. He has a double ad-
vantage. He has used the traditional poetic devices to great
effect in a highly-charged sequence. If the modern reader can
take it, well and good. If the modern reader rejects it, the
poet is quickly at his side, agreeing. In either case, we feel we
are once more back at the beginning, face to face with the
anarchic words which resist being knocked into shape. The
poet breaks through to an even intenser immediacy. 'The
poetry does not matter' (*EC* 71). The poetic question itself
(which was used to establish immediacy) is now brushed out
of the way as an obstacle to immediacy and (since the reader,

* The device of sharing with the reader the problems of composition
even in the act of composing is not of course new (one might argue
that Fielding utilizes the same device in his successive introductory
chapters to the books of *Tom Jones*), but it has been employed in novel
ways recently in the attempt to eradicate the illusionary element from
literature and to escape the fettering conventions imposed by limited
systems of contrived plausibility. In drama this attempt to eradicate or
play down the illusionary element (probably in the long run a vain
attempt, but that is another question) has been at the back of numerous
experiments. Thus Samuel Beckett has virtually tossed into the arena
of discussion between actors and audience the very questions which
illusion and naturalistic plausibility require one to keep at bay. So long
as this kind of discussion remains central to the poetic or dramatic
experience itself (as it does in Eliot and Beckett) the device is both
potent and valid.

by virtue of the poet's skill, swallows the paradox) an even starker, franker 'present' is established in which person and person confront one another, no longer really poet and reader, because poetry has been swept under the carpet as an intrusive artificiality.

The November disturbance falsified expectations. The expectations were that life could have a pattern at the level of 'succession', season following season in a rhythmic flow, so that the summer heat would be succeeded by the autumn calm, the pressure of man's prime by the serenity of his advancing middle age. Middle age was supposed to bring calmness and wisdom to compensate for the loss of vitality and thrust. Instead has come the disturbance of a misplaced spring, threatening a degree of derangement cataclysmic in its effects and implications. Middle age, experienced from the inside, proves so different from what it looked like and sounded like when in youth one was in contact with the 'quiet-voiced elders' that one is led to speak of a massive deception. Was it simply a deception of the young by the old, or a self-deception by the old? Is the one thing handed on from generation to generation, from middle age to succeeding middle age, simply the recipe for sustaining and transmitting this deception? Is the outward 'serenity' of the ageing only a contrived posture of inertia and moribundity calculated to maintain the pretence of age's wisdom – and to conceal the truth from self and from others; namely that advancing years reveal the uselessness of worldly experience and wordly knowledge for interpreting life's meaning, for achieving insight into the mystery of being, into the nature and purpose of what is, above all into the significance of the approaching darkness of death? The arrangement of ideas here seems to suggest that in the last resort the key pretence of the ageing is a pretence in relation to the fact of death – from which they turn their eyes.

It is important to follow closely the implicit logic of Eliot's assertions here: his exactness must always be fully reckoned with. Since the November disturbance has brought to us a realization of the falsity of the neat pattern of significance traced at the level of mere succession, the November disturbance, though shocking, was neither unhealthy nor unfruitful. Indeed it has proved revelatory, like the moment in the rose-garden, in that it has established the irrelevance of the familiar humanistic reading of life in terms of progress and positive temporal development. Thus Eliot now decries, as of 'limited value' at best, that 'knowledge which is derived from experience'. It is true that such knowledge reduces experience to order and therefore, superficially, 'imposes a pattern'; but the pattern is a false one, for it objectifies so neatly that it irons out the living 'moment', the illuminating present.

Eliot seems to be saying that the conventional picture of the human life-span, in terms of youth, growth, maturity, and age, as matching the seasons of nature, has no valid meaning. That is to say, the individual's course through life, viewed naturalistically, makes nonsense. For the individual has no *meaningfully* authentic relationship to the cyclic world of nature in which season follows season in the harmonious dance of rhythmic change, contrast, and movement. The supposed 'dance' of personal life (birth–growth–mating–breeding–decline–death) is not a 'dance' at all, humanly speaking, for it breaks down, collapses under the weight of disturbances which *are themselves more meaningful* than the superficial pattern which they disturb. If one is honest, and refuses to keep up the conventional deception of one generation by another, one has to reject the notions of progress by development and of meaning acquired by smooth gradations. The true pattern is 'new in every moment' (*EC* 85). Every moment enriches, not by steady addition to our understanding of life, but by shocking us into a new valuation of all that we have previously experienced. In so far as there is progress by succession in the world of understanding, it is self-nullifying because of the very character of 'succession' itself; for the illusions which we shed today are illusions which deceived us yesterday about yesterday and would anyway no longer have power to deceive us today about today. Today is different. We deceive ourselves in *thinking* that we make progress, for our minds are fixed on the seen-through deceptions by which we misled ourselves yesterday and consequently are unaware of the new and different deceptions protecting us from authentic response today.

This almost Proustian theme (it is relevant to recall Eliot's very high estimate of *A la Recherche du temps perdu*), which seems at first sight to reduce experience to a status of such relativity as to be nihilistic, is rescued from the Proustian pessimism by the transcendent religious significance which Eliot allows to his revelatory moments. Proust's illuminating moments of involuntary memory, which enable him to recapture and reconstitute the past, and thus subvert the tyranny of time, are ultimately of purely aesthetic significance. Eliot's 'moments' have a value and authenticity which is rooted in the Catholic framework of doctrine and practice to which they are related. Moreover, Eliot's criticism of the doctrine of progress on the intellectual front has corresponding implications on the moral front too, as we shall see in the next movement (*EC* 124 ff.) and elsewhere. (See especially *DS* 199–202.)

We are always 'in the middle'. Eliot echoes Dante whose *Divine Comedy* opens with the words 'In the middle', presenting us with the poet at the mid-point of his life-span, lost and bewildered, having wandered into a 'dark wood' (*EC* 90). Eliot intensifies the image by bringing Conan Doyle (*The Hound of the Baskervilles*)* to the aid of Dante (and thus exemplifying his own theory of how the ancient and the modern, the traditional and the contemporary, should be blended in a living literary idiom; see *LG* 220).

---

* The allusion may seem incongruous, though the God–Dog correspondence occurs in *The Waste Land* (see p. 142) as it does frequently in Joyce's *Ulysses*. The particular associative link here may well be traced through Thompson's *The Hound of Heaven*, with its 'following feet' and its 'footfall' (cf. p. 8).

Not only in middle life but throughout life we are lost in a
dark wood. And not only is the wood dark and a tangle of
brambles about us, but we are on the edge of a mire, our
foothold is insecure, and the threat of lurking monsters, and
strange deceptive lights, adds to our peril and our fright.
The account of life's insecurity given here rises to a climax
with the most awesome (and superficially most absurd) fear
of all, the risk of 'enchantment' – the possibility of the reality
of the preternatural. Indeed the words chosen – 'grimpen',
'monsters', 'fancy lights', and 'enchantment' – are powerfully
evocative of a state of mind whose very ambiguity is precisely defined. The overtones carried by this vocabulary are
just such as to leave us deeply unsure whether what makes
itself felt as surrounding the dark path of life with possible
mystery and dimensions unreckoned with, has that fanciful
preternatural character which the rational mind can afford to
laugh off and discount, like the terminology of a fairy tale,
or is laden with a challenge from a valid Other whose
demands we have evaded and habituated ourselves to ignore.
(Hound of the Baskervilles or Hound of Heaven?*)

It is against the habituating and deceiving character of old
men's assumed pose of calm and understanding that the poet
turns his anger. Now, when he has seen how hollow is age's
conventional claim to poise and wisdom, indeed how totally
false in view of the fact that the posture can be maintained
only on the basis of refusing to take the challenge of
approaching death into account, he denounces the folly of
old men. Their false posture is rooted in the fear of admitting
their fear (of death), rooted in their refusal to respond to the
challenge which the closing-in of finitude's horizons inevitably presents to them, the challenge to find peace by
giving themselves in love to another, to others, to God.
There is no true peace to be found in hedging ourselves
about within the false posture of eventide assurance and
understanding, when every minute brings us nearer to the
night of death, when every revelatory moment compels a

* See also p. 88 and p. 142.

revaluation of past experience in whose light the notion of progressively increasing understanding is shown to be nonsensical. Eliot has now finely dismantled the whole of our machinery for thinking in terms of progress by development and acquisition. The framework of reasoning at the social or personal levels in terms of a shapely, rhythmic human lifespan lies in ruins. Revelatory moments of true consciousness have in one way or another punctured our familiar umbrella of protective, habitual half-thinking, and we are exposed to the devastating realization that the only wisdom to be acquired is that of 'humility'. For humility is 'endless' in the double sense that it reaches out of time, rejecting the temporal life-span pattern, and that it eschews the selfish pursuit of worldly 'ends'.

The houses are all gone under the sea

Patterns established at the natural level alone will not do. The 'houses', the buildings and families whose existence we pictured in terms of cyclic succession are themselves swept away, disintegrated into the natural elements from which they sprang. The 'dancers', the human beings whose existence we pictured in terms of cyclic succession (and to whom we gave the empty meaning of a false patterning at the level of repetition, of a false stability at the level of the perpetually recurring) are likewise disintegrated into the earth from which they sprang. It is not by way of man's affiliations to the natural that one can reach a discernment of the meaningful dance in which he must take his place. The dance lies deeper. There is a paradox to be swallowed before one arrives where the true dance is. It is a parallel paradox to that which led us through darkness to light. The way is through stillness.

'So the darkness shall be the light, and the stillness the dancing' (*EC* 128).

The disappearance of the houses and dancers of history and of dream-history anticipates the disappearance of stage scenery (and of dancers too, perhaps, if we consider also *LG* 184) in the next movement (*EC* 116–7).

III

O dark dark dark. They all go into the dark

Leaving the personal present, the poet re-plants himself once more, this time in the civilizational present. He echoes Milton's words from *Samson Agonistes*. So doing, he assumes the stance of the prophetic poet passing judgement upon contemporary civilization. He sees the public life of his day as a procession of supposedly important figures from military, commercial, cultural, political, administrative, and industrial spheres. All are going into the dark, all marching death-wards – 'the vacant into the vacant', for their worldly status conceals an inner emptiness, and the death to which they move is conceived by their civilization only in terms of emptiness. (For clarification of 'interstellar', *EC* 102, see p. 77.) The cultural paraphernalia which they carry with them, as being what they have valued on earth, is represented by volumes of reference. This is the truly representative library of decadent civilization – not the works of great poets or thinkers, or even the encyclopaedias which might open doors to truth, but directories which *place* men and women in terms of social rank, and which guide one in the financial and commercial worlds. These strictly utilitarian books reflect the materialistic basis of our culture. Clinging to them, modern man, in whom true human sensibilities have atrophied and true human motivation has died, moves towards the 'silent funeral' (no kingfisher *answering* 'light to light' here). We are ourselves involved in this funereal procession, whose character does not even have the dignity of the tragic, for it is a corpseless funeral. This climactic touch – of the ironic and the farcical – should not be overlooked, especially by those who are tempted to think that the sharpness of the young Eliot's sting is missing from his later work.

The movement of civilization is wholly funereal, wholly deathward, yet there is 'no one to bury', for in the deepest sense we have died already – or rather we have never lived, never tasted full consciousness, for 'to be conscious is not to be in time' (*BN* 84) and we are locked within the temporal by our blindness to, or rejection of, the revelatory moments (and the doctrinal and institutional system within which their interpretation is contained and their recognition guaranteed).

This vacant darkness is fit only for the vacant. The Poet/prophet speaks again as witnessing, not taking part in, the procession. 'I said to my soul, be still' (*EC* 112). We must withdraw from the deathward march of contemporary civilization. We must seek a deeper darkness than the darkness of vacancy – the darkness which is found on the way of abstention from movement, on the way of discipline, of negation; for this is the 'darkness of God' (*EC* 113).

Eliot describes the discipline of withdrawal from the deathward march in three images, each charged with suggestive overtones. In the first image contemporary life is a stage show. The image conveys the ultimate impermanence both of the natural background, the 'hills and the trees' (*EC* 116), and of the civilizational background, not even solid buildings, but a 'bold imposing façade'. In the sudden darkness between the scenes one is aware that these are being rolled away. Conversational idiom appropriate to an account of a theatregoer's common experience is enriched by phrases ('movement of darkness on darkness') which add a religious dimension to it. The powerful ambiguity of the word 'wings' (with its angelic overtones) strengthens the sense that in the moments between the scenes we have an apt analogy in miniature for the possible winding-up of the whole natural order. With his customary skill, without 'preaching', Eliot has momentarily dangled before our minds the faint, barely recognizable question – May it be that a 'rumble of wings' in a mounting darkness will one day prelude the rolling up of the map of time?

In the second image contemporary life is once more a journey on the Underground, as it was in Movement III of *Burnt Norton*. The unexpected pause between stations, which is extended until conversation dies away, brings to light the 'mental emptiness' normally covered under movement and talk. The two go together (movement and talk) as distractions from the stillness and silence requisite for disciplined self-offering to God. (The fear of possible impending emergency, which always intrudes into the mind when the pause between stations lengthens out, is implicit in the 'growing terror'.) Thus in the first two images imposed darkness, stillness, and silence have withdrawn us momentarily so that we sense the emptiness of contemporary life as a false (theatrical) show and a meaningless journey.

The third image is the briefest but perhaps the most telling. The moment of withdrawal from the deathward march is like the first minutes under ether. We are now in the anaesthetist's hands. The full weight of the situation will be felt only when we have assimilated what follows in Movement IV of this *Quartet*. We are about to be operated upon. It is not enough to sum up our condition, when we withdraw from the procession, simply in images of men lost or bewildered in a sudden darkness, or stillness, or silence; lacking the familiar comforts of the illuminated show, the mechanical rush forward, the ceaseless chatter: for we are invalids. But the further exploration of that theme is reserved for the next movement. Notice, however, how the three images complement one another. In the first it was the impermanence of the natural and civilizational scene which was brought home to us. In the second it was the emptiness in the lives and minds of our fellow-travellers through time which was stressed. In the third we have the personal purgatorial experience of consciousness bereft of the objective distractions by which it habitually blinds itself to reality. From being momentarily aware that the world about us may be 'nothing' and the people about us have 'nothing' to think about (in each of these cases we are in fact aware of something), we become ourselves directly aware of 'nothing'. Obviously the line (*EC* 122) must terminate in a dash and the theme be dropped, or the poem would have to come to a full stop. How efficiently the anaesthetist has done his job we shall observe in the next movement.

Meantime our withdrawal from the deathward march is demanding, both morally and spiritually. It is not just a case of separating ourselves intellectually from the worship of progress and worldliness in a materialistic age. We have to cleanse ourselves of the false postures which pseudo-morality and even pseudo-religion urge upon us to boost our self-sufficiency. We must divest ourselves of hope which, in the vulgar sense of the word, is reliance on things turning out well for ourselves (or indeed for others) in the future. This kind of hope would be 'hope for the wrong thing', that is, for satisfaction or fulfilment, for improvement and well-being, in temporal affairs. Christian hope demands the laying aside of this kind of 'hope'. It involves a trust which would survive the defeat or disappointment of all earthly hopes. (Indeed we know from *Murder in the Cathedral* that even the hope of martyrdom or redemption, as an anchorage for the self's confidence or assertiveness, must suffer the same sacrifice.) In the same way we must divest ourselves of love which, in the vulgar sense, means pursuit of a desired object or attachment to a desired person as the provider or guarantee of one's own happiness. Christian love demands the transcending of this kind of love. It is centred in a principle of self-sacrifice by which what guarantees one's own happiness must not be cherished on those terms. Faith alone, which is wholly undemanding as a personal attitude, is our sustaining principle – and 'love' and 'hope' in so far as these virtues, Christianly understood, cleansed of all elements of desire and therefore of all *movement* towards a wanted future, constitute a condition of 'waiting' (*EC* 126).

The moral and spiritual disciplines have their intellectual corollary. We must 'wait without thought'. Eliot has striven in many paradoxes to define for us the necessity of the intellectual humility which he saw was contradicted by the prevailing humanistic philosophy of progress. Poet as he was, he strove to convey this insight, not polemically, but as part of a living experience of truth which, having known, he must share. What makes us (as yet) 'not ready for thought' is the assertion of self-sufficiency implicit in the intention to think things out, as we say.

It is probable that Eliot assumes a special connection between the pause between the scenes and waiting 'without hope' (that there will necessarily even *be* another scene to follow: for any moment may be our last: see *DS* 124, the reference to Krishna's words quoted in *DS* 156–8). Likewise it is probable that Eliot assumes a special connection between the pause between stations and waiting 'without love'. (For 'love', in the easiest, cheapest sense, might here lead us to the kind of consolatory act which merely boosts other people's distractedness from what they ought to be facing. That is to say, if out of compassion we start up a conversation in the silent tube, we merely revive the empty talk which prevents people from facing the emptiness of their lives and the unreliability of their familiar world.) Thus the state of submission to the anaesthetic is parallel to the reliance upon faith alone. In this condition we shall indeed wait 'without thought'. We are going to put ourselves into the surgeon's hands. Only when he has finished with us shall we be ready for thought.

And then? The 'darkness shall be the light, and the still-ness the dancing'. The true light is found in the darkness between the acts when the artificially illuminated show is temporarily suspended: the meaningful movement (pat-terned and orderly) is discovered in the stillness when the pointless mechanical journeying from station to station is temporarily halted. At such points of suspension, when we are withdrawn from the deathward march, we may attain to new moments of revelation. The images in which these glimpses of illumination are contained carry rich overtones. 'Whisper of running streams' certainly brings back from

Burnt Norton the theme of air alive with noises, of air patterned into half-recognizable utterance, and also evokes a contrast with the silent, static, painted scenery that has been rolled out of the way. 'Winter lightning' points forward to the renewal of revelatory experience in old age, giving us one more instance of the meaning which cuts right into the human course as lived in slavery to the seasonal pattern of cyclic Nature, establishing again, in terms both of poetic form (for it looks forward to *Little Gidding*) and of personal autobiography, the truth that future as well as past are gathered into the truly meaningful present. 'Wild thyme unseen' and 'wild strawberry' (*EC* 130) suggest sudden un-covenanted revelations of two kinds – those given in poetry through the experience of others (since 'wild thyme' is pre-sumably Shakespearean), and those given directly in per-sonal experience. All these, and the 'laughter' and the echoes from the garden of *Burnt Norton* (not to mention John Donne and his 'ecstasy' already echoed), gathered together (for they are 'not lost'), demand and point to the central Christian paradox of coming to life through death. The two verbs 'require' and 'point' (*EC* 132) balance each other neatly: for the revelatory experiences at the same time make clear the need for human self-surrender if they are to be in the long run more than tantalizing glimpses of fulfilments which temporal life fails by its inevitable limitedness to provide, and yet also themselves give one a hopeful taste of the joys of true birth lying on the far side of death. The textural precision represented by Eliot's use of the word 'point' is quite remarkable. In *EC* 47 ('Dawn points') we found the same verb used to mark the repetitive daily cycle as *compelling* us forward in the ultimately meaningless (and mechanical) process of 'succession'. The contrast here is powerful. As dawn pointed to one more stage in the death-ward march within time, so the revelatory moments (which occur during the suspension of servitude to the temporal) *point* out of time to the birth beyond death.

You say I am repeating

The paradox that the way to new life is through death is now explored in a series of incantatory sentences which echo a passage in *The Ascent of Mount Carmel* by St John of the Cross. The sentences give different versions of the indivi- dual's need to discipline himself by self-surrender in order to achieve true self-fulfilment. The repetition is insistent and appropriate. Its effect is crucial to Eliot's message; namely that life time and again hammers the same truth into the fabric of man's experience. If you wish to arrive where you truly and fully exist (not just partially, 'living and partly living') and get away from the twittering world (*BN* 113), the 'place of disaffection' (*BN* 90), then you must discipline yourself along the way of negation rather than directly and consciously pursue the kind of 'ecstasy' whose echoes you have caught in the given revelatory moments of illumination and joy. If you wish to have knowledge of the truth, you must turn aside from the self-centred acquisitive pursuit of fact and mastery, represented by humanistic culture, and accept the limitations of human ignorance: you must empty the mind of the assertive grasping after information and open it to the silence. If you wish to possess what you lack, you must learn to dispossess yourself; for it is the possessive and possessing self which, distracted by its own possessive- ness and enslaved to its own acquisitiveness, hinders you from self-emptying and self-opening that is the necessary prelude to possession of what alone is worth possessing. Likewise, if you wish to become the true *you* which you now fail to be, you must go by the way in which the false 'you' (the assertive, claiming, knowing, possessive 'you') is negated, cast off, and ceases to be.

Three summary paradoxes round off the incantation, and each of them is reversible. 'And what you do not know is the only thing you know' – What you, as an assertively knowing creature do not claim to be in possession of as knowledge is precisely the true knowledge which is alone worth having. The point of your admission of ignorance is precisely the point of your entry upon knowledge. 'And what you own is what you do not own' – That which you truly possess is that over which the acquisitive 'you' asserts no possessive claim. Conversely, what you claim possessively for your own is precisely that which the true *you* cannot possess; for assertive ownership is slavery to that which we imagine we own. We think we possess when we are being evilly possessed; when we learn to possess nothing we shall be truly and fruitfully possessed. Lastly, 'And where you are is where you are not' – Where the true *you* fully exists is where the self-centred 'you' has abandoned all its claims, has ceased to be. Or, conversely, where the consciously assertive 'you' exists is precisely where the true humble *you* cannot really *be*.

IV

The wounded surgeon plies the steel

Our human situation is now summed up more concretely, the paradoxes translated into symbols. Care must be taken over the interpretation of these symbols. For Eliot's symbolic correspondences, though often precise, are not exclusive. No harm is done by identifying precise symbolic correspondences precisely, provided that exclusiveness is not claimed for the identification. With this proviso we approach a lyric whose theological reference is notably sharp. Man's situation is described in symbolic terms which, paraphrased, clearly re-express the doctrines of Original Sin, Grace, Redemption, and Atonement.

We are patients in a hospital in the hands of the operating surgeon. The surgeon, himself wounded, is plainly Christ, whose sharp scalpel probes our own wounds, thereby paining us. Our sufferings are the probings of the one who alone can heal us. They are thus, for all their sharpness, the product and the sign of the divine compassion. The word 'questions' (*EC* 148) carries overtones of torture, which powerfully reinforce all that has been said in the last movement against the adequacy of merely consolatory religious values to sustain us in the face of disillusionment with our civilizational background and our naturalistic heritage. (Cf. *LG* 207. 'Who then devised the torment? Love.') That the surgeon's own hands are 'bleeding' guarantees the authenticity of the healer and his art. He will not submit us to more than he has himself borne. And the operation is directed to clearing up the worrying irregularities of the temperature chart above our bed. These irregularities, of course, express the incompleteness of our adjustment to the cyclic course of the natural order to which we are temporally bound. It follows that our 'only health is the disease' (next stanza).

We have spoken against exclusiveness in interpretation of symbolic correspondences, and indeed it is important not to miss further parallels imposed serially on the foregoing account of the first stanza. The words 'plies', 'steel', and 'questions' carry distinct overtones, literary rather than clinical. As we read this poem, the poet, himself wounded as we are wounded, probes with his pen the 'distempered part' of our own lives, making us face the questions he has faced – for his hands are bleeding. (In so far as the horoscope hinted at in *BN* 54 is a 'fever chart' documenting our hospitalized condition on earth, the Cross alone can resolve its 'enigma' – and the enigma also of that questioned, 'distempered part' of the poem, *BN* 47–61. See App. III, 5.)

Our only health is the disease

The fact of disease – the recognition of ourselves as being diseased and under treatment – represents the only healthy aspect of our condition. The paradox is multifold. As we have said, our defective adjustment to the measurable operation of the cyclic natural order (as marked by our irregular temperature chart, recording the pointed moments which, upwards or downwards, all but take us out of time) is the proof of our affiliation to another, supernatural order.

Moreover, identification of disease (where it has not been recognized) represents identification of true health (for which it has been mistaken) and is thus the first step to the recovery of health. If we obey the 'dying nurse', the Church, who is constantly reminding us that we are diseased, and whose duty it is thus to disturb our complacency (rather than to 'please' us), the hope of true health is real. The Church, in reminding us that we are diseased, is merely reiterating that the human race lies under the curse of Adam, is suffering from that inner tendency to evil which is technically called 'original Sin'. The optimistic aspect of this allegedly pessimistic doctrine must be noted. The doctrine stresses that the deficiencies of human beings and human societies, over which we worry so much, represent, not humanity in a state of health natural to his true, God-given human condition, but humanity in a state of unnatural disease. The point is relevant to Eliot's paradox. If we are to be restored, our false assumption of health must be eroded by acceptance of our sickness.

The whole earth is our hospital

Man's situation on this earth is thus that of a patient in a hospital. The image directly challenges prevailing humanistic and scientistic notions of human independence and progress. We are under treatment. Whether the 'ruined millionaire' who has endowed our hospital is primarily God the Creator who has poured out his resources on our behalf, or Christ who ruined himself in order to share his inheritance with all mankind, or Adam whose fall virtually squandered a fortune, is arguable. The overtones suggesting resources poured out generously in providing for human needs are evident, but the image of a patrimony squandered by the Fall of Man occurs in Sir John Davies's *Nosce Teipsum* –

> 'How can we hope, that through the Eye and Ear,
> This dying Sparkle, in this cloudy place,
> Can re-collect these beams of knowledge clear,
> Which were infused in the first minds, by grace?

'So might the heir, whose father hath in play
Wasted a thousand pounds of ancient rent,
By painful earning of one groat a day,
Hope to restore the patrimony spent.'

Later in the poem Davies deals with the apparent injustice of
disinheriting all 'the unborn nephews, for the father's (i.e.
Adam's) fault', and of advancing again 'for one man's merit
(Christ's)/A thousand heirs that have deserved naught'.

'And is not God's decree as just as ours,
If He, for Adam's sins, his sons deprive
Of all those native virtues, and those powers;
Which He to him, and to his race did give?

'For what is this contagious Sin of Kind,
But a privation of that grace within,
And of that great rich dowry of the mind;
Which all had had, but for the first man's sin?

'If then a man, on light conditions, gain
A great estate, to him and his, for ever;
If wilfully he forfeit it again:
Who doth bemoan his heir? or blame the giver?'

The extent to which Davies tussles with this theme (there is
more of it yet) is of interest in view of Eliot's known attachment to his work. But Eliot's emphasis is upon our dependence as beneficiaries and patients, watched over by an
'absolute paternal care'. The words here describe an authoritative divine Providence which overlooks all our doings, and
is omnisciently present with us at all times. If it forestalls all
our earthly efforts and hopes directed towards temporal
health and well-being ('prevents us everywhere', *EC* 161),
it does so by *anticipating* our deeper and more lasting needs
(for 'prevents' is used also in the Prayer Book sense). We
shall 'do well' under this paternalistic regime if we resign
ourselves to die. It is the ego that must die, the self that sins.

The chill ascends from feet to knees

The account of our human suffering which is given here is of the 'purgatorial', sacrificial kind by which, along the way of negation, we learn to deny ourselves – to die unto sin. To some extent the imagery appropriately inverts that in which the affirmative experience of reconciliation was described in *BN* II. There the blood danced along the artery and we felt the warm sap 'ascend to summer in the tree' (*BN* 55). Here the 'chill ascends from feet to knees'. There the sensitive 'trilling wire in the blood' under old wounds was insulated by appeasing scars ('Sings below inveterate scars', *BN* 50). Here is a very different kind of singing, that singing in the head which marks a fever. Although Eliot does not explicitly make the parallels, overtones and associations give the 'trilling wire' of *BN* 49 perhaps a primarily musical connotation (cf. the violin note of *BN* 144), while the 'mental wires' here more surely recall humming telegraph wires. (Telegraph wires belong to the compulsive thrusting roadway–railway image-cluster as violin strings belong to the still, patterned work-of-art image-cluster). The word 'chill' brings the taste of death back from *BN* 132 as well as the flavour of winter. The chill's ascent up the legs will gather overtones from the *Titanic* disaster (App. III, 4) as well as from prayer in draughty churches (*BN* 87 and *LG* 45).

If we are to find true warmth and health, then this gradual freezing of the self by which the soul learns to die unto sin must be fully endured. The paradoxes of fire and frost are pressed upon us in their negative aspect, as they were in their positive aspect in 'winter lightning' (*EC* 129). Even the feverish quaking must be replaced by frigidity (as the 'destructive fire' gave place to the reign of the ice-cap, *EC* 66 and 67). The freezing, flaming purgatorial fires may have a Miltonic sting, but in Eliot the fire-frost paradox is essentially part of the total blended textural-theological network which has given such unity and coherence to his imagery as a whole. (For instance, the birth-death paradox in the *Journey of the Magi* must continually recur to the mind of the reader of the *Quartets*, as must the opening lines of *The Waste Land*. Our commentary takes up this theme at greater length when it has gathered still further enrichment. See especially p. 174.)

The last line of this stanza should be noted by all those who have tended to over-simplify Eliot's exploration of the Way of Affirmation and the Way of Negation. There are not two ways but one. And yet there are two ways. These truths too are paradoxical. Naïve systematization is dangerous. Here at the heart of a lyric whose emphasis is upon discipline, self-sacrifice, and the acceptance of suffering, the climax of the purgatorial imagery plants roses at the centre of the freezing, cleansing fires. The sharp thorns are the smoke. If one penetrates the choking cloud and steps right into the flame, it turns out after all to be what (in view of the hospital atmosphere) one is tempted to call a bed of roses. (Readers of George Macdonald's *Curdie* books will recall the fire of roses in *The Princess and Curdie* – and will indeed often have cause to ask themselves how much Eliot may have owed to the detailed symbolism of Macdonald.)

The dripping blood our only drink

The imagery of the Mass used here brings us what is perhaps the clearest and most specific religious equation so far demanded by Eliot's metaphorical scheme. The supernatural life, the life enjoyed by the healthy world outside, for which our temporary earthly hospitalization prepares us, can be sustained here and now only by the food and drink which nourishes us in membership of Christ – the body and blood sacrificed for us and given to us in the sacrament. This is our hospital diet. It is the only thing which keeps us alive in our sickness. In spite of this truth we deceive ourselves that we have a solid substantial existence as purely natural beings, independent of our supernatural status and vocation. As mere creatures of flesh and blood, our claim to health and soundness is a false one. As creatures of Nature we are both sick and insubstantial. The theme of the opening of the

lyric is implicit in its ending. Only through recognition of
our inadequacy and sinfulness as fallen children of Adam can
we find the cure we need. Good Friday, the day on which the
surgeon was wounded (the 'steel' pierced his own side also)
and his hands bled, brings us knowledge of the extent of our
sickness and of the sacrificial cost of its cure, and yet still we
call it 'good'. The affirmative and joyful content of the
doctrines of the Redemption and the Atonement has been
effectively re-expressed for the modern world in living
imagery of the hospital and the operating table.

V

So here I am, in the middle way, having had twenty years –

Eliot speaks again with the voice of the professional poet – as
he did in the corresponding Movement V of *Burnt Norton*.
But though the discussion of the poet's experience in the
traffic with words establishes this link as between quartet and
quartet, the experience described makes a more material link
with the second part of Movement II of *East Coker* (81 ff.).
There we noted the poet's Proustian reflection that in so far
as there is progress by succession in the world of understanding, it is self-nullifying because of the very nature of
'succession' itself; for the illusions which we shed today are
illusions which deceived us yesterday about yesterday and
would anyway no longer have power to deceive us today
about today. This reflection, made at the personal level, in
terms of man's progress through middle age, is here paralleled in the poet's more technical experience *qua* poet, that
is *qua* practitioner with words. 'In the middle way' (the
phrase brings back Dante* again; see *EC* 89 ff.), in middle
age, the poet is aware of years wasted in the vain attempt to
learn how to use words. One does not make progress as a
poet by successive stages of growing mastery over the verbal
medium. There is no step-by-step development for the

* For fuller consideration of Eliot's indebtedness to Dante see p. 146.

practitioner in poetry. One always starts afresh from scratch and each time one fails in a different way. In so far as one eventually gets mastery over words, it is only in relation to the things one no longer wants to say and in a fashion of speaking in which one no longer wishes to speak. Today's practitioner finds that he has mastered only that mode of utterance which he wanted yesterday and is not relevant to today's needs.

Thus one is always making a fresh start and never building on successively-mastered stages of development. Every new 'venture' in the struggle to achieve valid poetic utterance is a 'new beginning' in which one is, as it were, making a raid upon the terrain of inarticulacy (in the hope of establishing some fresh outpost of articulacy). But in making one's forays into the domain of inarticulacy one is always conscious that one's equipment is deteriorating. One sets out to establish a firm position of effective verbal utterance, only to find that one's own linguistic resources (needful for the task) are themselves corrupted by the general infection of imprecision and indiscipline which the current climate of pseudo-literacy spreads. The experience of the craftsman in words thus parallels that of the ageing individual who has learned that 'every moment is a new and shocking/Valuation of all we have been' (*EC* 86–7).

Eliot of course finds in the history of poetry and in the practice of poetry the most effective possible instances to support his assault upon time-ridden notions of progress. In the field of poetic utterance it is obvious that 'what there is to conquer . . . has already been discovered'. Virgil does not improve progressively on Homer, Dante on Virgil, Shakespeare on Dante, Milton on Shakespeare, Eliot on Milton. Each poetic masterpiece represents a new start and a different kind of failure. The masterpiece is the product of 'strength and submission' – of individual labour and fresh poetic power on the one hand: of submission to the discipline and nourishment of the literary tradition on the other hand. (This balance is important, as we see in Eliot's more detailed investigation of poetic utterance in stylistic terms in *Little Gidding*, 216 ff. It is also of course in tune with his attitude to the relationship between individualism and authority in other spheres.) One cannot regard the great poet either as standing on the shoulders of his predecessors or as competing with them. The poet struggles – not in order to improve upon his predecessor's achievement, still less to rival it, but rather to 'recover' what he found – what has been found and lost again in the creation and subsequent ageing of every valid poetic utterance. The poet struggles to build again in his own day the needed bulwark of articulacy achieved. And the conditions for such achievement seem highly 'unpropitious'. The word is a potent one – potent by virtue of Eliot's superb mastery of the idiom of calm, scholarly understatement transmuted into poetry. The final judgement is that judgement cannot be passed on the poet in terms of gain or loss. The poet's task is to keep on trying. 'The rest is not our business.' Line 189 is characteristically rich in extra overtones. 'For us, there is only the trying' means both that we can only try to do our best, and also that we are thus on trial. 'The rest' is not only *what remains* but also the rest as opposed to the movement (the usage represented by saying 'The stone is at rest') and rest as opposed to work ('Day of rest'). That is to say, the stillness at the centre is not 'our business' – but God's (our 'Father's business'). The rest, the still point by reference to which what moves and turns is finally shown to be patterned and meaningful, is not an *end* we can pursue. Thus the poet's task and vocation as poet is in perfect correspondence with his personal vocation as ageing man. He stands within the lineage of great poets as he stood within the lineage of the human family, learning to acquire the 'wisdom of humility'. For 'humility is endless' (*EC* 98).

Home is where one starts from. As we grow older

The notion of 'home' as the secure resting place to which one finally returns in the evening of life is false to the facts of human experience. Like other sentimentally false patterns which delineate man's earthly span in terms of a rhythmic curve, the notion is disproved by experience. Home is rather the starting-point than the last resting place. As we grow older we do not find that life gradually familiarizes us with an increasingly congenial and increasingly intelligible environment. Indeed when we reflect on our experience, the underlying pattern which we do discern is one which age renders more, not less, complex. And this is not only because the interconnectedness of current experience proves more tangled than we might have expected: it is also because the interconnectedness of human experience turns out to involve the dead as fully as the living. Thus the 'intense moment' in whose revelation we found the pointer to true pattern and meaning cannot be fully interpreted in the mood represented at the end of *Burnt Norton* –

> 'Ridiculous the waste sad time
> Stretching before and after.' (*BN* 174–5)

The note on which the poet ended *Burnt Norton* over-emphasized the isolation of the revelatory moment through stressing the contrasting emptiness of the waiting time before it and after it. The very intensity of the moment's illumination is itself a 'gathered intensity' (to employ Browning's phrase in a way) on which is focused the significant experience of a lifetime. More than that, because of the nature of human consciousness and the character of the collective tradition which it is nourished on and which it preserves, there is focused on to this same revelatory moment the significant experience of lifetimes of the past – not just the known historical past, but the far past, not yet understood, but dimly recorded on the undecipherable fragments of lettered stone.

The implicit correspondence with what has been said in the previous section about the work of the poet is important. Just as *Four Quartets*, the masterpiece, contains the gathered intensity of Eliot's experience, holding personal past, present, and future within its patterned revelation, so that Eliot's lifetime burns in it; even so *Four Quartets* contains, once more 'recovered', the gathered intensity of Milton's lifetime, Dante's, Virgil's, as already 'discovered' (Go back to *EC* 183 now to savour the full ambiguity of this word – *revealed*) in *Paradise Lost*, *The Divine Comedy*, *The Aeneid*. Thus the masterpiece in literary history is like the intense moment in personal history. Both are revelatory. Both have an intensity which, while it superficially separates them from the current 'before' and 'after', holds the packed experience of past lifetimes. Both the literary masterpiece and the intense moment puncture the natural cyclic sequence, disturb the pattern of the seasons, and defy the 'laws' of progress by succession. Both have hidden depths and unexplored dimensions by virtue of the gathered intensities of lifetimes present and past which they contain. Both 'recover' what has been 'discovered' (uncovered) and lost again repeatedly. Both feed and are fed by the traditions in whose context they can alone be understood. (And here we use the word 'tradition' in its widest sense – the sense in which language, meaning, and reason are traditions, things transmitted from age to age in the communal human consciousness.)

Having made these weighty correspondences, Eliot once more checks the argument before it reaches the stage of seeming to denigrate negatively the natural sequence of life from youth to age which is our inescapable lot. There is a time for both the 'evening under starlight' (*EC* 197) and the 'evening under lamplight' (*EC* 198). Both have their place. The two images are complementary. The evening under starlight is the memorable time of youth; the evening under the lamplight is the remembering time of age. The two images of light carry overtones linking them with all the moments of illumination scattered throughout the poem. (And these 'moments', from the heavily symbolic, like the revelatory glittering in the *Burnt Norton* garden, to the briefest glimmer of 'winter lightning' – *EC* 129 – are all thematically interconnected. Each has *some* degree of symbolic reference, however slight.) Here the natural 'starlight' balances the artificial 'lamplight'. In each moment human experience is brought within range of that *influence* (the word deserves a firm, almost medieval connotative reading here) which lightens our darkness by puncturing the straight progress of the temporal. Because 'star' in *The Dry Salvages* is associated with the Virgin Mary and therefore with the Annunciation by which the eternal breaks into the temporal, 'starlight' inevitably carries overtones that identify points of intersection of the timeless with time. Hundreds of love-lyrics speak of the young lovers' sense of eternity experienced under starlight. It is scarcely necessary to press the vast literary exploitation of the star symbol from the days of Beatrice to the days of Molly Bloom. Remember that the deathward march of the vacant into the vacant led into the starless 'interstellar' spaces (*EC* 102).

'Love is most nearly itself' in those moments when, planted in our respective chronological phases of life – youth or age – we are yet lifted out of the temporal by the 'starlight' romanticism of young love or the 'lamplight' reminiscences of age. At such moments 'here and now cease to matter'.

The conclusion, that old men 'ought to be explorers', is not of course a reversion to the blinkered doctrine of progress. The exploration required of the old is not an exploration in range but in depth. 'Here and there does not matter.' It is not a case of moving over the surface of space. Rather we stay still and thus move, not into another locality, but into 'another intensity'. The plunge is to be from dimension to dimension in pursuit of further union and deeper communion. We have to plumb more profoundly those gathered intensities of present and past, personal and historic, which give the revelatory moment or the revelatory masterpiece its sureness and its power. 'Union' and 'communion' alike are words with strong personal, literary, and religious force, designed to be equally applicable to the individual surveying his autobiographical lot, the poet surveying his professional task, the Christian surveying his vocation. The search for the filling out of the additional dimensions and for the further clustering of gathered intensities is the search for pattern and for meaning which, whether in personal, literary, or religious life, is 'discovered' at given revelatory moments and 'recovered' by the exercise of 'strength and submission'. The willed way of recovery is of course the negative way of discipline, so we face the 'dark cold and empty desolation'. The imagery of the sea on which the old must set out inevitably recalls Tennyson's *Ulysses* if only because the poem is actually echoed in *The Dry Salvages* ('The sea has many voices . . .' *DS* 24). The 'vast waters' here seem to represent the very bounds and farthest reaches of the natural and the temporal, inhabited by us and – beyond the limits of man's history – by animal creation ('the petrel and the porpoise'). Our pursuit of the 'deeper communion' will take us – voluntarily in mystical contemplation and involuntarily at death – over the borders of the natural and the temporal. In this sense man's earthly end is his beginning. But the last sentence of the poem has other meanings too, for it signifies the completion of the circular pattern of the poem, *East Coker*, which itself constitutes a *recovery* (cf. lines 1, 14, and 50). And the true 'end' of the poem is the reconstitution of a pattern disturbed and a fabric crumbled; the restoration of a fallen 'house'.

The Dry Salvages

I

I do not know much about gods

The river represents the flow of Nature, within us and about us, the dark god which man has to subdue in civilizing himself and his world. The imagery matches an American river, altogether bigger, browner, more formidable, less friendly, than its English counterpart. Clearly we are back in Eliot's home area of St Louis, Missouri, beside the Mississippi. The description of the god as 'sullen, untamed and intractable' makes clear that the poet does not regard twentieth-century man as having subdued the powerful natural forces as effectively as he thinks he has. We sense that the dark god's apparent submission is a deception and, as often in Eliot, awareness of the precariousness of our civilized condition is compressed into an understatement of terrifying calm – 'patient to some degree'. To what degree? How far can we go? The implicit questions are worrying.

The first recognition of the river 'as a frontier' must be read in the light of the peculiar American usage of the word 'frontier' for the area which forms the border of a country's settled and inhabited regions over against its improperly explored and subdued ones. And one must recognize the implicit correspondences between world history, American history, and the individual's life-story, as the account of man's struggle with Nature proceeds. Thus, in the course of human history, awesome awareness of Nature in the fringe area of the yet knowable and controllable, is succeeded by a stage in which the natural is used but not yet thought of as mastered ('useful, untrustworthy', *DS* 4), indeed treated with the respect and wariness which the word 'untrustworthy' carefully suggests. The third stage is that in which the river has become nothing more than 'a problem confronting the builder of bridges'. Superficially the natural appears to have been mastered, but in fact it has not been gripped and harnessed; rather it has been by-passed. The development has been such that the true character of the natural has been ignored. Man imagines that the 'problem' has been 'solved' (*DS* 6). The deceptive finality of the foolish, arrogant phrase (accorded nothing higher than a parenthetical status) aptly identifies the superficial confidence of our urban civilization in ignoring and underestimating the power and vitality of Nature. The god is not dead; neither is he domesticated or appeased. 'Implacable', he pursues his seasonal course within us and about us, likely at any moment to rage or destroy.

The sense that our mechanized culture presses forward under an ever-impending threat from the deep natural forces which it has but supposedly subdued and is now vainly trying to forget, is expressed in that fine generalized Eliotian idiom which renders the judgement applicable to our current condition over wide areas of social and personal experience. Eliot is not the kind of poet to make specific references to bombs or cancer of the lung or modern neurosis or mass-production, in order to press home his point. The choice phrases, 'dwellers in cities' (*DS* 7) and 'worshippers of the machine' (*DS* 10) are all that is necessary to make us feel small and fearful (Are there not overtones of Sodom and Gomorrah?) over against the 'waiting, watching' (*DS* 10) power which we have for so long ceased to respect.

The flow of Nature within us and outside us, binding our lives to the cyclic rhythm of the seasons, is referred to here (*DS* 11–14) in images which again recall those of the affirmative experience in *BN* II. There the flow of blood, and perhaps of semen, were by implication linked with the flow of sap in the tree and the 'drift of stars' in the sky (*BN* 54–5). Here the flow of urine 'in the nursery bedroom' (*DS* 11) marks our involvement with the untamable, flooding life of Nature as surely as does the flow of Molly Bloom's urine in

Ulysses. In the 'rank ailanthus of the April Dooryard'* we probably have a symbol of the overflowing of the sexual river in the spring of life. Eliot seems to pin both the animal and the romantic aspects of youthful sexuality by combining the word 'rank' with the word 'ailanthus' (the tree of heaven with a phallic connotation). His purpose is neither to denigrate nor to idealize the natural, but to see its paradoxical duality. The potentially uncontrollable profusion of the ailanthus is an apt symbol for the sexuality of adolescence or young manhood ('April dooryard' gives us the season of life), but the threat that our natural affiliations offer to our civilized human status is not peculiar to any one age. If the urination of infancy and the sexuality of youth remind us of the bondage to nature which we try to forget, no less threatening to our civilized balance is the bouquet from the wine-glass which tempts us more in the autumn of our lives ('the smell of grapes on the autumn table'). And finally the sentimentality of age (for surely, in line 14, in 'the evening circle in the winter gaslight', we are back at the 'evening under lamplight' of *EC* 198, turning the pages of the photograph album) is no less certainly a link with the flowing, liquid life of Nature, for one may take it that the old folks' reminiscences cause the tears to flow. Thus, at various stages of life, our bondage to Nature may be re-asserted in the uncontrolled flow of urine, semen, drink, or tears.

Our interpretation here relies on an assumed correspondence between four ages of life and the four seasons. The justification for this assumption is firstly that the correspondence is a commonplace of Elizabethan thinking about the ordered universe, on which Eliot depends in his use of Elyot, Sir John Davies, Shakespeare, and others; secondly that a correspondence of this kind is explicitly made, for instance, in *EC* 74-5 ('the autumnal serenity/And the wisdom of age'); and thirdly that the same kind of

* There is an echo here, as also in *DS* 47-8 and *DS* 182-3, from Walt Whitman. See p. 113.

correspondence seems to be implicit in the imagery of *LG* 1–20, and again in the imagery of *EC* 51–67. The fact that the correspondence here, in *DS* 11–14, is drawn between Infancy, Adolescence or Young Manhood, Middle Age, and Old Age on the one hand, and a pre-Spring phase, Spring proper, Autumn, and Winter on the other hand, will not weaken the force of our reading for those who are familiar with the liberties taken by Elizabethan writers themselves with their own accepted system of correspondences. Discrepancies in parallelism are commonplace in the literary tradition we are exploring.

The four instances chosen at this point to represent our physical links with the flowing life of untameable Nature are perhaps intentionally all instances in which relief and satisfaction is experienced as physical needs are answered. They seem to be obliquely referred to again in *DS* 90–2, where the poet distinguishes between revelatory moments of happiness and mere experiences of satisfaction produced by fruition, fulfilment 'or even a very good dinner'.

The river is within us

The poet re-plants us locally. We move from the river to the coast. Eliot has himself identified the place for us. It is the coastal area near to the city of Gloucester, Massachusetts, where a lighthouse stands off Cape Ann. (In view of cumulative nature of the coming symbols it is worth noting that St Ann was the mother of the Virgin Mary.) We should remember that Eliot's father had come to live in St Louis in 1834. Before that date the Eliot family had been in Boston, Massachusetts. When the poet left home in St Louis to study at Harvard (Boston) he was returning to the 'home' area where many families such as his had been established since they emigrated from England in the seventeenth century. (Thus the move was the first in that series of steps to 're-covery' which later took Eliot back to residence in England and burial at East Coker.) Some thirty or so miles from Boston is Cape Ann and the City of Gloucester, one of the

most important fishing ports and markets in the world. It is
also of course a centre for the manufacture of fishing gear
and for boat-building. The fishing centred on the city of
Gloucester is clearly in the poet's mind at many points in the
first two movements of this *Quartet*. It is no doubt relevant
that Gloucester was founded in 1623 by settlers, many of
whom came from Gloucester in England. It must perhaps
remain a matter for conjecture whether this connection
caused Eliot to choose the name of a manor house in
Gloucester for the title of his first poem, *Burnt Norton*.
Readers might see significance in the choice of a manor
house garden in Gloucester, England, as the scene of a
might-have-been past. Eliot, associating the city of Gloucester, Massachusetts with the flow of natural life and the
flux of history which moved families like his own from
England to Massachusetts and thence to Missouri, might
logically choose the corresponding English area for the
location of a might-have-been childhood in which all was
ordered and patterned, the family presences of the past and
the future (echoes of the now dead and the laughter of children yet to be born) together blended with a present in
which all were 'accepted and accepting', *BN* 30. We must
bear in mind throughout that the *Burnt Norton* garden is the
might-have-been Paradise of ordered family life which man
might have enjoyed had there been no Fall, cosmic, or
historic, or personal – no human rebellion to cause the
ejection of Adam and Eve from Eden, no ideological
quarrels, religious and political, such as brought about the
emigration of Puritans and dissenters from England to
America. Eliot's American upbringing is, for poetic purposes, in a 'strange land', and is symptomatic of man's
alienation and homelessness. His search for roots is both
literary and geographical, personal and social. We do not
impose these parallels on the poems: they are implicit in the
imagery. For the religious quarrels which caused English
families to emigrate to New England (as Eliot's family
emigrated), and which came to a head in the civil strife of the

seventeenth century, are touched on later in *Little Gidding* (cf. pp. 123–4), and imagery throughout the *Quartets* which speaks of wounds healed and wars appeased (*BN* 50–5 and *LG* 191) is thus interconnected in the total network with hints of an 'ideal' family history in which the movement of emigration (as symptomatic of a disorder destructive of the hierarchical dance) need not have taken place. Later overtones fill out this network of correspondences by linking the cost of civil strife in martyrdoms with the Crucifixion (*LG* 176, and see pp. 161–2), and by threading into the theme of past strife and its healing, echoes of the American Civil War (see p. 113).

It is not easy to draw the line between reasonable interpretation and fanciful conjecture at those points in the poem where perceptive reading makes one aware that Eliot is both hinting at, and shrouding, personal memories, but the preoccupation with his family's own history of movement, here evident, certainly throws a new light on the images of the might-have-been past conjured up in *Burnt Norton*. We may here add that Eliot's earlier lyrics, *New Hampshire* and *Cape Ann*, are quoted in *Burnt Norton* and *Little Gidding* (see p. 182) in such a way as to support our view of the elaborate thematic inter-relatedness which makes it possible to see the 'formal pattern' in the 'box circle' (*BN* 31–2) as alluding to an imaginary family history unbroken by emigration. Be that as it may, the symbolic use of the New England coastline and the sea in the present movement certainly throws back significance upon earlier sea images. Thus we can now (only now, I think) understand why the poet, having spied on an archaic dream picture of patterned family life among the rural dancers of *East Coker* I (27 ff.), thereafter quickly transferred his stance from an English country lane to a coastline ('Out at sea the dawn wind . . . I am here/Or there, or elsewhere', *EC* 48–50).

The sea, which is 'all about us' represents, as it did at the end of *East Coker* (*EC* 208), the ages of time stretching out before and after the human span. And here we use the words 'human span' both of the individual's history and of the history of the whole human race. It is important to grasp this concentration of meaning in the symbol: for the sea appears to be, not just time as it ebbs and flows tidally through the lives of men and families, but the inconceivable, virtually limitless scope of the temporal, stretching backwards and forwards beyond the range of human comprehension. In this sense the sea becomes a symbol of the very bounds and farthest reaches of the natural and the temporal and, as such, in its distances is lost in the eternal.

The sea of time bites into the granite edge of the land on which we stand, the earth of which we felt ourselves fashioned in *East Coker* I. It tosses up relics of history and pre-history. The picture of beaches littered with souvenirs of past life, animal and vegetable, and likewise with pathetic remnants of past human effort and action (fragments of net, lobsterpot, and oar) is sharply reminiscent of the *Proteus* episode in *Ulysses*. In view of this close resemblance, it is significant that the repeated phrase 'many voices' echoes Tennyson's *Ulysses* –

'The deep
Moans round with many voices. Come, my friends,
Tis not too late to seek a newer world.'

That Eliot's ancestors set out to seek a newer world is sufficient to account for the fact that Eliot found Tennyson's lines memorable: but we should note too that there is a later reference to Penelope (*DS* 41) and that Tennyson's poem came to mind at the end of *East Coker* (see p. 78).

One is probably justified in saying that faint sexual overtones once more reinforce the correspondence between the flow of water in river and wave and the tidal flow of sex through human history. 'It tosses up our losses' perhaps hints at the costly wastefulness of our self-expenditure in sexual as well as other activities. Certainly the 'torn seine' is a highly charged image, for 'seine' is of course the breast and Eliot has already, in *Murder in the Cathedral*, used

85

the word 'torn' with peculiar sexual sharpness in the phrase

> 'the torn girl trembling by the mill-stream'.

One might reasonably argue too that the phrase 'torn seine' with its inevitable and logical echo of the Latin 'sinus' has a Virgilian flavour and that Dido, along with the Virgin Mary and Eve, has her place in the multiple archetypal symbolism of womanhood underlying the thematic framework of this poem. Be that as it may, we must stress here the first mention of ocean wreckage (*DS* 22–4) and the introduction thereby of a theme to which the imagery of *DS* II, and many later scattered overtones, will add gradually and cumulatively until finally the articulate recall ('recovery') of actual historical disasters is achieved, and the external 'menace' of the uncurbed natural force about us is concretely asserted. (See App. III, 4.)

The underlying 'menace' of the uncurbed natural force at work *within* us is most powerfully asserted, as Raymond Preston first noted,* only when we reach the firm thematic statement of *DS* 101–3, in relation to which the imagery here may be likened to the premonitory figures and phrases which in musical form may anticipate the emergence of a clearly articulated subject or a fully-drawn melody. For indeed the imagery of broken remnants represents the souvenirs of a primitive racial past, which the retentive subconscious throws up fitfully into the waking consciousness, just as it represents the débris of a personal and individual history.

The salt is on the briar rose

These two images concisely remind us that all which grows and represents the beauty and joy and fruitfulness of the natural, rooted in the soil of earth, yet flourishing and flowering in the higher element of air, does so under constant threat from the destructive, erosive moisture blown

---

* Raymond Preston, *Four Quartets Rehearsed*, Sheed & Ward, London, 1946.

from the sea of time (the third element, water). The touch of bitterness which this tyranny introduces into human experience of love and beauty is symbolized by the 'salt' on the rose. The blur of mist and confusion which the steady passage of time introduces into human action and enterprise seems to be symbolized by the 'fog' in the 'fir trees'. It would seem that the overtones of the first image are feminine, of the second image are masculine (if one uses the terms 'feminine' and 'masculine' rather of different fields of human interest and action than as strictly sexual differentiae).

The sea howl

The two voices that are thrown at us from the sea of time (the sea of history) and the sea of eternity into which it reaches are distinguished as 'howl' and 'yelp', the one a threatening and frightening cry, the other perhaps rather a cry of pain. As we look out over the ocean of history, these two very different cries come to our ears, often at the same time – for the very experiences of man's past whose recall worries and threatens us most are often those in which men suffered most (the wars and turmoils, tortures and disasters recorded in history). These two voices have already been hinted at in the last line of *East Coker*, 'The wave cry, the wind cry' (*EC* 208). As the waters of time and the winds from the waters of time beat age by age against the land in which man's natural family life is rooted and against the frail vessels in which he launches himself for business and exploration, the cries that arise from the resultant constant struggle between humanity and time reflect the nature of the struggle. That there is pain and irritation to endure in man's struggle is sufficiently clear from the image of the 'whine in the rigging'. Something of the threat concealed under time's movement when she seems least inclined to interfere with our condition (when the waves of time are not actually touching us, but breaking over themselves), is caught in the line, 'The menace and caress of wave that breaks on water', (*DS* 29). The corrosive effect of time on even the toughest of the earthly foundations on which men stand is heard in the 'distant rote in the granite teeth' (*DS* 30) as the winds and waves grind remorselessly at the indentations of the coastline. (Gloucester granite is famous. Cf. *DS* 16.) Thus with images of whining, grinding, and wailing, along with terms like 'menace' and 'warning', Eliot builds a strong verbal fabric to stand for the unceasing tale of struggle and pain, insecurity and fear, that is constituted by man's historic encounter with ravaging time.

We are, however, concerned with a struggle whose dimensions extend farther still. We may note that 'howl' and 'yelp' and 'whine' of *DS* 26, 27, and 28, are the voices of a Dog – and consequently, maybe, of a God. That is to say, they re-echo the threat of the 'monsters' (Hound of the Baskervilles or Hound of Heaven? See pp. 56–7) which 'menaced' our way (*EC* 92) in *East Coker* II, as the wave here brings its divinely paradoxical 'menace and caress' (*DS* 29). The fuller significance of this cluster of connected hints and echoes, carried indirectly but unmistakably in the secondary overtones of the text, will emerge only if we take into account the line to follow in Movement V,

'To report the behaviour of the sea monster' (*DS* 185).

In drawing out the full content of this allusion it will be appropriate to quote a paragraph from the *Hampshire Chronicle* of 29 June 1968. Under the heading, *150 Years Ago*, an interesting item is salvaged from the débris of the past – the issue of 29 June 1818.

'*London* – Captain Woodward, and the mate and seamen of the schooner 'Adamant' which arrived at Hingham on Sunday last from Penobscot saw in the afternoon of the previous day, about twelve leagues east of the Cape Ann, a sea-serpent, apparently upwards of 100 feet long which frequently raised its head a considerable height from the water. It was very near the vessel for about five hours; a full view was had of it, and it appeared to be about as large as a barrel but no protrudances were noticed. It was fired at and appeared irritated by the explosion. Depositions were preparing at Hingham to be sent to Boston for publication.'

That the sea off Cape Ann should be the scene of a reported appearance of a sea monster establishes a link between already related clusters of overtones all hinting at that intermittently audible challenge of the preternatural or the supernatural which fitfully disturbs our waking or half-wakeful consciousness, especially when we are 'lying awake' (*DS* 40) 'between midnight and dawn' (*DS* 43).

Eliot presses farther the blended threat of the elementally natural and the incursive supernatural which always menaces our daily course of living and partly living in his richly suggestive symbolic treatment of the bell, which rings its warning from the reef to safeguard seamen who may be lost in the fog. For the bell, like a voice from outside time, speaks to us of a steady rhythm deeper than the breaking and bluster of wave and wind. The bell becomes an important symbol for the rest of this movement and its significance is carried over into the succeeding movement. It will help the reader if we anticipate what is to follow by identifying at least one of the correspondences which the symbol of the bell gradually gathers. The bell is the bell which will toll our deaths (*DS* 66). Thus the bell measures a time older than clock-time: it marks off measurements much bigger than those which sleepless women count off as they listen to striking clocks during the night; for it marks off life from death, the temporal from the eternal. The bell tolled by the groundswell, therefore, represents an 'unhurried' undercurrent beneath the normal tidal movement of time. (Cf. the word 'unhurried' here with Eliot's use of the word 'hurried', *LG* 86, and our comment on it, p. 143.) Since the word 'groundswell' is used especially of movement caused by distant storm or even seismic disturbance, it is especially appropriate to signify those indications of cataclysmic (or revelatory) temporal/eternal 'intersection' which may be experienced when we are withdrawn from hearing the usual clamour of history's 'sea voices'. In this connection, notice that Eliot uses the word 'ground' later with overtones from Julian of Norwich (the divine Ground – 'the ground of our beseeching', *LG* 199). Here the emphasis seems to be on the bell's reminder to *us* that we must each die.

But that emphasis is not exclusive. Through the night, like anxious women, we worry over the future and re-trace the past. The words 'unweave, unwind, unravel' echo Joyce and show that Penelope was in Eliot's mind. Penelope, waiting for the return of her lost husband, Ulysses, put off the pressing suitors by agreeing to marry one of them when she had finished weaving the shroud for Laertes, Ulysses's father. At nights she unravelled what she had woven during the day. The apparent reference to Penelope coincides with previous recollections of Ulysses (*DS* 24). Moreover the scene of Sir John Davies' poem, *Orchestra* (see pp. 17–18) is set at Penelope's court. The argument that the dance is the principle of all order, harmony, and culture is voiced by Antinous the suitor, and addressed to Penelope in the attempt to persuade her to join in. Joyce's Penelope, of course, weaving and un-weaving her mental fabric of past and future during the quiet hours of the night, breaks off to count the strokes of St George's clock. Thus into the image of human beings hearing the fearful reminder of mortality there is here compressed the notion of fobbing off a challenge by delaying tactics. The Penelopes here, waiting for the Great Wanderer's Return, have something in common with the Women of Canterbury. Sexual and spiritual overtones blend in the choruses of *Murder in the Cathedral* (there is more to be said about this on pp. 175 ff.), establishing a relationship which needs to be taken into account in reading *Four Quartets*.

We have not yet done with the unweaving, for Eliot's personal pilgrimage back from St Louis to Massachusetts, to England, to East Coker (and to the might-have-been Burnt Norton) represented an attempt to 'unweave, unwind, un-ravel/And piece together the past and the future', and, in *East Coker*, it was 'between midnight and dawn' that he watched his dream-picture of the Eliot ancestry dancing round the fire (*EC* 25 ff.). That 'the past is all deception' (*DS* 43) in this period of 'dim light' (*BN* 92 ff.) 'before the morning watch' (*DS* 44), which is neither day nor night (neither daylight 'investing form with lucid stillness' nor 'darkness to purify the soul', *BN* 92 and 96) we have already understood. But Eliot is full of paradoxes. There are deceptions and deceptions. The 'deception of the thrush' (*BN* 22) proved a fruitful one to follow: the deceptions practised upon us by our elders (*EC* 75) proved ultimately powerless to deceive.

However, the elaborate symbolic construction *concealed here gradually acquires a sharpness and distinctness as we move towards the second and climactic sound of the bell. Eliot has taken the superstition that a mysterious bell is heard at sea when disaster approaches. He has blended this with the image of the 'groundswell' which also foretells danger. By playing with the ambiguity of the word 'ground' (the Divine Ground 'that is and was from the beginning' *DS* 46) he has once more associated the symbols of distant and approaching menace with the challenge of the Supernatural that men dimly sense in those moments of sudden insecurity, when the habitual support of the familiar and the routine is withdrawn. Time and again, in order to instance this kind of moment, Eliot uses the experience of sleeplessness in the middle of the night, when time seems to stand still, when brooding makes the past look disillusioning and the future hopeless. The echo in line 43 of Psalm 130 ('My soul fleeth unto the Lord: before the morning watch, I say, before the morning watch') is richly appropriate. The psalm begins, 'Out of the deep have I called unto Thee, O Lord'. The threat here comes from 'the deep', and the following lyric is perhaps Eliot's most moving cry *de profundis*.

* See App. III, 3 for further multi-dimensional readings.

II

Where is there an end of it, the soundless wailing

As in the corresponding lyrical sections opening the second movements of *Burnt Norton* and *East Coker*, the feeling is here conveyed that a distinct and acute personal experience lies behind the suggestive imagery. The reader cannot escape the impression that this lyric deals with the poet's assimilation of a real calamity – an '*agony*' as intense as the moments of joyful illumination previously recorded.

The bell foretelling death is now established as a symbol marking the point of intersection of the timeless with time. It announces our mortality. But the bell is used by the Church on other occasions than the funereal. It is used daily to ring the *Angelus* and recall the Annunciation – the angelic announcement to the Virgin Mary that she was to be the mother of the Saviour. This Annunciation, pointing to the divine Incarnation, heralds the archetypal historic inter-section of the timeless with time. The established association of the Virgin Mary with the sea makes her presence in the background of the *Dry Salvages* as fitting as the presence of Christ in the background of *East Coker*, where the theme of Our Lord's suffering in the flesh was appropriate to the dominant concern with the element earth and man's rooted-ness in it. The association between water and the feminine is of course a constant with the symbolists. The Virgin is directly addressed only in Movement IV, but her presence is felt here in the repeated use of the word 'annunciation', in the specific reference to her response to the Angel Gabriel (*DS* 84), and perhaps in the shape of the lyric. (Each pair of lines appears to represent one toll of the bell. Three threes and a nine are rung for the *Angelus*.)

The *Angelus*, like the death bell, brings the sudden chal-lenge of the temporal–eternal relationship before us. It is perhaps relevant to add, in view of the direct references to the Eucharist in *EC* IV, that a bell is rung in the sanctuary (and sometimes in the tower) to mark the moments of

Consecration. The point at which bread and wine are declared the Body and Blood of Christ is clearly another point of intersection of the timeless with time (cf. *BN* 87).

As is the case with the corresponding lyrical passages in *Burnt Norton* and *East Coker* it is impossible to know the autobiographical detail behind these moving stanzas, yet the note of personal authenticity is unmistakable. The particularity does not perhaps matter; the personal authenticity does. We seem to hear speaking a middle-aged man from whom the possibilities of joyful and revelatory emotional life are dropping steadily away, like falling petals, while he remains 'motionless'. The emphasis is upon a drying-up of life's positive promises, which is faced in a mood of death-like immobility and unresponsiveness. The total and over-powering nature of the defeat or disaster is such that it leaves one incapable of emotional resistance (even the wailing is 'soundless') and likewise incapable of submission to Providence by prayer. The sense of loss imaged by the 'drifting wreckage' and the 'bone on the beach' combines associations of defeat and bereavement, which strip the spirit bare of worthwhile possession, interest, or bodily delight. (In view of later, unmistakable allusions to Shelley, it is difficult for the reader who is acquainted with Trelawny's recollections of Shelley and Byron to avoid thinking of Shelley's end when reading lines 52–3. Cf. pp. 99 and 143. There are praying bones, however, in *Ash Wednesday* II which take us back to *Ezekiel*. To follow this particular link would lead us, as so often in tracing Eliot's allusions, to a complex network of related literary references.)

There is no end, but addition

Stricken by calamity which he cannot immediately assimilate in prayer, the poet finds no 'end' – no purpose and no cessation – in what remains. He is himself for a time in that fettered condition upon which judgement has so often been passed in this poem. He exists temporarily in servitude to mere succession. The prospect before him is of meaningless 'addition', hour to hour and day to day, requiring him to adjust himself by atrophy of emotional sensitivities to a continuity of empty existence, surrounded by shattered hopes. The things he most trusted in have been taken away from him. The logic of this is sadly noted: they were the things most fitting to be removed if he was to be disciplined to 'renunciation'.

There is the final addition

It is characteristic of Eliot's poetic practice that a neat philosophical distinction should be made at the very climax of this deeply emotional lament. In the stricken life, a man cannot look for an 'end' (which word always implies roundedness and purpose in this poem). Rather he foresees only the 'final addition', the last stage in the successive running-down of existence. This appears to be the final decay of emotional responsiveness, when even pride dies, so that one cannot even resent the fading of one's own capacities. One reaches a stage of negative detachment when devotion is so devoid of objective as to be virtually non-existent. The image of the last days before death is of a man drifting in a leaky boat, waiting for the dismal call of the death bell.

Where is the end of them, the fishermen sailing

With the end of the three threefold chimes and the beginning of the ninefold chime there is an appropriate turn in the thought. Up to this point we seem to have been listening to a personal lament on the loss of hope and the gradual approach of death. After this point we are looking out more impersonally on the lives of men in general, seeing them as fishermen continually setting out on their voyages and asking what is the 'end' (purpose and conclusion) of their continual toil. What do their lives *mean*? The efforts and risks of men's ceaseless toil to survive are pressed upon us in the images of the wind's tail and the cowering fog. Surveying the continuing struggle, we find it impossible to conceive of true end or conclusiveness on this level of thought. That is to say, as long as we stick to the idiom of succession, seeing history in terms of continuity and addition, we shall never arrive at a rounded meaning. Rather we shall look out on an oceanlike stretch of time littered with the relics and waste of the past, and foresee a future that has no finality. There will be no point of 'destination' at which purpose and conclusiveness will be realised. (The word 'destination' contains a play on the word 'destiny'.)

We have to think of them as forever bailing

So long as we conceive of time (or history) as a great ocean on which the voyage of life takes place – so long, that is to say, as we preserve our familiar concepts of lives as individual progresses-by-succession within a larger field of historic progress-by-succession, we shall be tied to a notion of meaningless, inconclusive repetitiveness. In other words, we shall have to think of men as fishermen who go on and on, struggling against the elements, bailing the water from their boats, hoisting sails, tugging at them to change direction, while the sea's own base remains changeless. One struggle follows another in life, though it is true that there will be intervals of rest and reward on the physical level, just as the fishermen dock, draw money, and dry sails between voyages. But this humanistic thinking in terms of progress-by-succession precludes the more fundamental (and religious) concept of life as a single voyage out of which one is going to make no profit for oneself and from which whatever one gathers is likely to be unfit for 'examination'. The use of the phrase 'making a trip' suggests that the religious view of life is in one sense a less solemn view than the humanistic one. One takes oneself and one's career – one's earthly well-being – less seriously. It also suggests that the main purpose of life is not to get something out of it. Life is not comparable to a money-making voyage. The voyager is not going to be paid in accordance with what he has made. (We are near to the message of the parable of the labourers in the vineyard here.) And in so far as one does accumulate something by earthly experience, what one thus acquires will not stand divine scrutiny at the end.

There is no end of it, the voiceless wailing

The last stanza reintroduces the more personal and individual note of the first three stanzas. The 'them' of *DS* 67 and 73 are no longer in the forefront of the mind but the 'it' of *DS* 49 and 79, and Eliot stresses 'is' in reading *DS* 79. On the level of the natural (for that is where the image of withering flowers places us) there is no 'end' (neither purpose, cessation, nor conclusiveness) to the human experience of pain and failure and decay. The paradoxical phrase 'movement of pain that is painless and motionless' defines the misery of life on the natural, humanistic level in terms of decisive negativity. The suffering whose correlative is apathy contrasts sharply with the fruitful sufferings of sacrifice and self-discipline. The one-way movement of decay, whose correlative is immobility, contrasts sharply with the patterned dance whose centre is a point of still intensity. Similarly the 'drift of the sea' is towards no discernible point of repose or conclusiveness. And it is necessary to make clear again at this stage how careful Eliot is to avoid a one-sided denigration of the natural. Here, in a lyric concerned to stress the inadequacy of the natural in itself to satisfy human beings and to provide them with a purpose and meaning of things, the 'drift of the sea and the drifting wreckage' image the meaningless process of haphazardness and decay which one experiences and witnesses within the natural order when emptied of significance from outside itself. But the natural can be filled full of meaning by virtue of the revelatory moments which puncture its framework at the points of intersection of the timeless with time. And therefore we must balance the 'drift of the sea' here against the 'drift of stars' in *Burnt Norton* (*BN* 54). There man's joyful fellowship in the natural – dance in the blood matching dance of the stars – was transfigured in an experience of positive and joyful illumination. In the *Four Quartets* as a whole the one 'drift' balances the other.

Here, however, the emphasis is upon the ultimate negativity and meaninglessness of the natural-in-itself, untransfigured by illumination. Where the revelatory moments are lacking, there is only the way of obedience and self-discipline. This is the demand which calamity and suffering impose. And the only positive response, which can find meaning at the heart of the apparently meaningless, is that response of complete humility and self-surrender to the apparently impossible demand – the response archetypally represented in the Virgin Mary's reply to the supernatural Annunciation: 'Be it unto me according to thy word.'

It seems, as one becomes older

What has already been said in highly-charged imagery is now repeated in a more conversational and direct idiom. Thus once more the poet starts again, true to his insistence that 'each venture/Is a new beginning' (*EC* 178), 'and every attempt/Is a wholly new start' (*EC* 174–5) and true to what he is even now saying, namely that meaning cannot be found in 'mere sequence'. The naïve view of the past as a prelude to the present, the view which traces pattern in the shape of succession and development is a 'partial fallacy' ('partial' in a double sense – *in part* a fallacy, and a fallacy based on prejudice or *partiality*). The popular mind, infected by ill-digested evolutionary thinking, seizes upon the philosophy of progress and development because it provides an excuse for 'disowning the past' – the historic past and the personal past. 'Disowning' is a packed word, sharply ambiguous. We are tempted to 'disown' the public past, the cultural past (dispossess ourselves of it by cutting ourselves off from tradition) and to 'disown' our private past (fail to 'own' up to it). We have to 'own' both pasts, feeding on the one, repenting of the other.

The poet has already established, but here repeats, that the true pattern of the past is to be found in the gathered revelatory moments of illumination. These are the moments of happiness – happiness as opposed to sheer physical and emotional satisfaction and well-being experienced through the answering of bodily or psychological need or appetite, like the need for self-expression, success, 'security or affection' (cf. *DS* 11–14). And the moments of happiness do not constitute a pattern through some principle of successive accumulation or aggregation. Indeed, when the moment of happiness has passed we are left, it has been said before, with a sense of 'waste' (*BN* 174). For the memory of the experience remains but its meaning eludes us. Thus the discovery of the 'meaning' is the key to the restoration of the experience. Here we reach the heart of the argument, the point which explains why poetry is necessary, why the *Four Quartets* were written. 'Approach to the meaning restores the experience/In a different form' (*DS* 94–5). To realize the meaning of the experience is not to recover it in the sense of achieving a repetition of the happiness which it brought. Rather to realize the meaning is to *restore* the experience in such a distinctive way that the issue of 'happiness' is transcended. When the past experience is thus 'revived' through arrival at its meaning, the experience (being now 'restored', that is, re-stocked, re-fuelled, re-victualled also) is seen to have gathered to itself the content of comparable experiences in the lives of our ancestors, and indeed carries unfathomable undertones from the remote primeval ages outside the reach of 'recorded history'. It goes without saying that the *Four Quartets*, in realizing the meaning of Eliot's past moments of happiness, have found them enriched by comparable experiences in the lives of his ancestry. And his ancestry is a multiple one. There is, for instance, the family ancestry represented by Sir Thomas Elyot and the poetic ancestry represented by Dante, Milton, and other poets (see *LG* 92 ff.).

Thus far the poet has been recapitulating the argument of *East Coker* V, but now a new twist is given to the argument, bearing on the fact that the *Dry Salvages* records how the calamitous has to be assimilated. What applies to revelatory moments of happiness applies also to 'moments of agony'. This is so, irrespective of whether the calamities are self-induced to the extent that they spring from our own mis-understanding in hoping for the wrong things or in dreading the wrong things (cf. *EC* 124–5). The implicit inference is that thus to set one's heart on 'things' beneath, not on 'things' above is inevitably to invite providentially cor-rective discipline: or rather, putting it another way, it is to court inevitably consequential disappointment and dis-illusionment. (The reiteration of the word 'things', *DS* 106, has a biblical flavour.) Moments of agony have the same kind of 'permanence' as moments of happiness. The illumina-tions and the agonies are alike part of the recurring ex-perience of the individual and of the human race. We can distinguish the pattern of meaningful recurrence more clearly in the agony of others who are close to us, and in whose suffering we therefore share, than in our own private calamities. Thoughtful reflection on our own personal sufferings is difficult because our own past experience of suffering is entangled with what we did, why we did it, and what resulted from it. In other words, remembered (and much brooded over) 'currents of action' blur the clarity of our past sufferings from our own eyes. But the calamities of others, whom we have personally known, can be dis-entangled from the subsequent trail of regret and remorse. Individuals recover from the shocks that have overwhelmed them and learn to smile again; but the agony they have undergone remains for us who know them as an ineradicable fact of their being. In this sense 'time the destroyer is time the preserver'. (The phrase echoes Shelley's *Ode to the West Wind*, 'Destroyer and preserver; hear, oh hear!' See pp. 93 and 143 for other Shelleyan echoes.) The river of time carries its load of lumber – the relics of past calamities. (It carries them away, time the destroyer; but it *carries* them, time the preserver.) And among the refuse of the calamitous past, along with the floating Negro corpses, 'cows and chicken coops' (with the tale of human cruelty and waste which they tell) there is carried the bitter and bitten apple; perhaps the apple of discord thrown into the assembly of the gods, which set in motion the train of events behind the Fall of Troy, and therefore behind the long struggle of Aeneas to recover the past and restore the fallen city (the burnt city); certainly the apple in the Garden of Eden, whose biting was the first archetypal act of human wickedness. Thus indeed the apple is itself a fragment from 'behind the assurance/Of recorded history' (*DS* 101).

The idea of the Fall, which the symbol of the apple introduces, is crucial to our understanding of the poem as a whole. In order to explore it we must cast our eyes backwards and forwards. At the end of *Little Gidding* we learn that the tree in the *Burnt Norton* garden in which the children are hiding is an apple tree (*LG* 248), and the paradisal status of the garden is reinforced. Thus the meaning of the allusion here to the 'bitter apple' is fully realizable only by reference back to the beginning of the first *Quartet* and forward to the end of the last *Quartet*. As we gradually approach 'the meaning' of the *Burnt Norton* experience, we hit on the recovered past which it contains, the past which belongs to Eliot's ancestry and the past which belongs to the whole human race. The *Burnt Norton* garden represented the might-have-been order of unbroken family life which generations of Eliots would have enjoyed had there been no religious and civil strife and subsequent emigration. Likewise it represented the Paradise from which human generations were ejected by the Fall of Man. The modern European-American's upbringing is, for poetic purposes, that of an 'alien' in a strange land, and therefore symbolic of man's upbringing on an earth shut off from ancient hierarchy and primal innocence. Every aspect of man's alienation, homelessness, and rootlessness is thus explored conjointly in this poem: and by 'every aspect' one means the religious, the historic, the racial, and the personal.

It is necessary to do full justice to the symbol of the apple here because the symbol in the next line is closely related to it. The 'rock' in the sea of time is of course the Church. The adjective 'ragged' is powerful. It refers no doubt to the unattractive roughness of the Church's exterior and probably also to the Church's superficial poverty, in that it suggests rags; but it also seems to echo Donne's *Good Friday, Riding Westward* where Christ's crucified flesh is described as 'ragged and torn'. (The seeming echo is worth noting because the poem contains usages of 'hurried', 'whirled', and 'restore' which appear to be echoed in *Four Quartets*.) The image of the rock, we are suggesting, carries the blended paradoxical associations of temporal threat and eternal security ('menace and caress', we might say) which are characteristic of Eliot's imagery of divine agencies and impulses as they intrude upon our steady routines. When we are confronted with the 'ruinous spring' beating at our closed doors in *Murder in the Cathedral* or with the 'ragged rock' in these 'restless waters' in which life's voyages are made, then we face that which 'itself the greatest destructive agony, constitutes the greatest preservation – the symbol of the perfected meaning, the eternal stability', as Grover Smith* says of this image. In fairweather times of prosperity and maximum calm the Church is 'merely a monument', something pleasant to look at perhaps, but useless. In navigable weather it serves as 'a seamark to lay a course by', providing guidance for those who choose to have regard to it, and perhaps appropriately definining the turning-points of life (with Christenings, Marriages, and Burials). As so often, one does not know quite how much to read into the correspondence, but the note of guidance and salvation is further strengthened if we pick up the hint of *Coriolanus* V, iii, 75 –

> 'Like a great sea-mark standing every flaw
> And saving those that eye thee!'

In times of suffering or of sudden calamity it 'is what it always was' – the indefinable destroyer and preserver.

* *T. S. Eliot's Poetry and Plays*, p. 280.

The echo of *Coriolanus* must be related to other Shake-spearean echoes hereabouts and elsewhere. Many of them are so slight in themselves as to make it seem improper at any given point to try to derive significance from them (cf., for instance the 'yellow leaves' of *DS* 128 and Macbeth's 'my way of life/Is fallen into the sear, the yellow leaf', *Macbeth* V, iii, 23–4), but we are dealing with a poet whose every syllable is weighed and with a poem in which meaning is to be found by the gathering in of scattered hints. Thus in *The Dry Salvages* generally the clanging 'bell' of *DS* 48, in close proximity to the image of sleepless women (*DS* 39) and to the word 'unravel' (*DS* 41 – cf. 'sleep that knits up the ravelled sleeve of care', *Macbeth* II, ii, 36) probably repre-sents an intentional addition from *Macbeth* to the number of presences about us – an addition which we shall perhaps have to take even more directly into account when the theme of the murdered or martyred king is articulated in *Little Gidding* (see p. 166). Meantime a more immediate con-cern is the apparent echoing of *Hamlet* in the phrase 'currents of action' (*DS* 111, cf. 'their currents turn awry and lose the name of action', *Hamlet* III, i, 87) and in the emphatic phrase 'and smile' (*DS* 114) to which we shall return later (see p. 167). Alongside the hint of *Coriolanus* already referred to (*DS* 121), these hints of *Hamlet*, and the probable hint of *Othello* in the allusion to 'dead negroes' (*DS* 116), together represent a faintly detectable cluster which performs at least three functions. In the first place, like the image of the apple, it involves the problem of evil with the problem of suffering. In the second place, it peoples the poem, adding faces, as it were, to the anonymous sufferers whose agony we share and learn from, and thirdly it strengthens the sustained parallel-ism between the experience of poetry and the experience of life.

III

I sometimes wonder if that is what Krishna Meant

There is reference here to the Hindu scriptures, the *Bhagavad-Gita*. Krishna exhorts Arjuna to acquire disinterestedness. Man must always act as if there were to be no tomorrow. The advice coincides with Eliot's warnings against living for the future and justifying actions according to their results. ('You argue by results, as this world does.' *Murder in the Cathedral*.)

The images here used to represent the future seem to have been chosen in order to put the future on a par with the past. Because the future is inside a book that has not yet been opened, because it is unknown, we idealize it, just as we idealize the past. The future we picture is in fact a sentimentalized future on a par with the sentimentalized past which is cherished in faded songs and souvenirs. The implication is that just as the past, represented by the heraldic emblem (the 'Royal Rose') or the dresses preserved in a drawer with a lavender spray (public past and private past: in the latter case the associations suggest a wedding dress), is a dream past, so likewise our contemplated future is a dream future, imaged with the same kind of nostalgia and melancholy with which we preserve our treasured souvenirs of the past. Wistful thoughts of future and past alike are directed to those who are not here at present. Whether they are not here because they have gone or because they have not yet come makes little difference. The word 'regret' could properly be used either of reminiscence or of anticipation, either of the past (with its might-have-beens) or of the future (with its might-bes). The centrality of the present is again established.

The centrality of the temporal present is inevitably represented by spatial imagery. Our terminology of the temporal has a spatial character. To speak of the 'philosophy of *progress*' is to employ a concept denoting movement in space. Eliot makes clear here, as elsewhere, that the full weight of

spatial reference is relevant when speaking of the centrality
of the present. He presses the full signification of the circularity symbol upon us once more. The way up and the way
down are the same. They are the same because, for Eliot,
centrality is not just an intellectual position (*vis à vis* the
philosophy of progress) and a cultural position (*vis à vis* the
poetic tradition and the need for perpetual 'recovery'); it is
also a moral position (*vis à vis* the selfish obsession with anticipated future or regretted past), and a spiritual position (*vis
à vis* the claims of 'the World': see *Murder in the Cathedral
passim*). The Way of Affirmation and the Way of Negation
are one way. The way of given illumination and the way of
self-discipline are one way. All this, and more, is implicit in
the single line,

> 'And the way up is the way down, the way forward
> is the way back.'

which might be used to exemplify the packed character of
Eliot's cultivated surface 'vagueness'. His most transparent
generalities direct the mind to a rich multiplicity of parallels
and correspondences. No reader should imagine that he has
exhausted them. We have certainly not yet here fully explored the content of this particular line. No doubt, in its
moral implications, 'the way forward is the way back' is also
a statement about the need for and the nature of repentance,
while in its professional poetic implications it might be said
to be perfectly illustrated in the fact that Eliot's craftsmanship achieves its maturest expression by drawing upon the
resources of past poets. Again, it might be taken too as a
direction on the proper way to understand *Four Quartets*;
and of course its personal biographical implications seem to
be evident in the long pilgrimage from St Louis to the village
of East Coker.

Eliot admits the difficulty of trying steadily to 'face' the
cluster of paradoxes which his doctrine of the centrality of
the present comprehends. Therefore he selects one instance
especially relevant in view of the emphasis upon personal

calamity in Movement II of this *Quartet*. 'Time is no healer' because 'the patient is no longer there'. We are reminded that the river of time is 'destroyer' as well as 'preserver' (*DS* 115). What time carries it carries away. We are also reminded of the hospital imagery of *East Coker* II. If 'the whole earth is our hospital' (*EC* 157) then indeed it is obvious that the earth's inmates (Staff apart!) will be patients. When the wounded surgeon has finished with us, we shall have died 'of the absolute paternal care' (*EC* 160). You do not find healed patients in hospitals. Eliot's sentence is something more than the inversion of a platitude into a paradoxical counter-platitude, partly because of the network of correspondences into which it fits and partly because of the further philosophical overtones carried by the word 'patient' – a word which Eliot elaborated richly in *Murder in the Cathedral*:

> 'They know and do not know that acting is suffering
> And suffering is action. Neither does the actor suffer
> Nor the patient act . . .'
> *(Murder in the Cathedral*, p. 22).

Thus Eliot's statement is not just a statement about the nature of time (that, in spite of its passing, 'the agony abides', *DS* 114), but a statement about the nature of true healing – and indeed of true action – both of which are out of time (see *Murder in the Cathedral* again:

> 'It is not in time that my death shall be known;
> It is out of time that my decision is taken
> If you call that my decision
> To which my whole being gives entire consent.'
> – Thomas's words, p. 79).

In so far as the patient is healed he is out of time. And in so far as he is healed he has ceased to be under treatment. No longer being operated upon, he has yielded his entire being in consent to the 'absolute paternal care' (*EC* 160) of which the patient dies. This is the only way in which we can 'do well' (*EC* 159).

Two further images are used for the purpose of dispelling self-deceptive attitudes to time (and progress). The first image, that of the train journey, has obvious links with *Burnt Norton* III and *East Coker* III. The passengers carry with them 'fruit, periodicals and business letters', the clutter and the future litter of tube and road and river (cf. 'Men and bits of paper', *BN* 104, and 'The bitter apple and the bite in the apple', *DS* 117). Though the journey offers 'relief' after the grief of parting, it cannot provide a symbol of true peace for the relief is a negative surrender to the drugged sleepiness of the measured hours beaten out by the mechanically rhythmic motion of the train. It is a shallow 'relief' which is purchased by indulging the false notion that one is escaping from the past (and its 'grief') and moving into a future which will be different. The sense of freedom thus purchased is illusory, for the idea of enjoying a present suspended in sabbatical respite between firm past ('that station') and even firmer future ('any terminus') is untenable. For one thing 'the narrowing rails slide together behind you'. The image takes us back to other images in which enslavement to selfish desire and temporality is similarly represented ('the world moves/In appetency, on its metalled ways', *BN* 124–5). The temporal journey, conceived in terms of escaping the past and riding cheerfully into the future, is made under compulsion (cf. *EC* 18, 'And the deep lane insists on the direction'). There is no continuity of identity between the imaginary self now *en route* and the self that left the past and will arrive at a future. This is because the journeying consciousness (suspended between the 'time before' and the 'time after', *BN* 91, supposedly moving 'from' and 'towards' *BN* 63) is not a true consciousness.

The second image, that of the voyage by liner, reinforces the first. The sense of mechanically determined movement is present again in the word 'drumming'. The word is powerfully suggestive, not only recalling the noise of the engines, but also subtly linking this voyage with the progress of family history whose picturesque image was conjured up by the 'weak pipe and the little drum' in *East Coker* (*EC* 26) and with a later reminder that we must not enslave ourselves to the historic process ('We cannot restore old policies/Or follow an antique drum', *LG* 186). The voice 'descanting' in the rigging (and thereby distinguishable from 'the whine in the rigging', *DS* 28, which is a voice heard clearly within historic time) is mysteriously above what the ear can hear (the 'murmuring shell of time'). The quality of this timeless, languageless utterance links it with the 'unheard music hidden in the shrubbery' of the paradisal garden in *Burnt Norton* (*BN* 27) and with the 'music heard so deeply/That it is not heard at all' in *Dry Salvages* (*DS* 210). What this voice from outside time has to say is again that to conceive a present in which one is *en route* from past to future is self-deception. The self thus artificially withdrawn from the temporal sequence in contemplation of supposed past past and supposed future future is an imaginary self, for 'you are not those who saw the harbour/Receding, or those who will disembark' (*DS* 150–1). But there is nevertheless a possibility of realized identity and true consciousness 'between the hither and the farther shore' (*DS* 152). If one is prepared to regard past and future 'with an equal mind', in detachment from all backward regret or forward desire, all sense of escape or of anticipation, and to accept in the present the eternal decisiveness of the present (as containing past and future), then one can receive the truth which validates the voyage through time. This truth is expressed in Krishna's words. The thought which treats the present moment as though it were the moment of death is doubly authentic in that every moment is the time of death (our only way of doing well, *EC* 159–60), and that the realization of this thought is the only fruitful action men are capable of. Not that one must realize this thought *because* it will be fruitful for others, for so to subordinate the present to results (and therefore to the future) is to cancel out by contradiction the very act of freedom from temporal enchainment in which one is engaged. Man must be purely 'intent' on that 'sphere' of being by which he is freed from servitude to successiveness. (One is reminded of Kierkegaard's dictum, that 'purity of heart is to will one thing'.)

O Voyagers, O Seamen

The effect of the break in the paragraphing at this point and of the direct address to voyagers and seamen is not only to add emphasis but also to shift the appeal on to a more personal level. Time after time in the poem Eliot adopts this device of making a 'fresh start' in a different voice. The fresh start is usually made in phrases which introduce a new degree of familiarity or intimacy at a point where fluency may have produced a sense of habituation that needs to be broken. The device is thus the poetic equivalent of re-personalizing one's conversation by breaking into one's own explanation, putting one's hand on to the hearer's shoulders and claiming fresh attention by a warmer approach. It establishes, at least for a moment, a sense of deepened personal contact and intensified sincerity.

In this particular case the device is especially potent for two other reasons. In the first place Movement III began on a ruminative, almost casual note, and only gradually has reflection ripened into exhortation. This new paragraph marks, as it were, the full accumulation of gradually gathered earnestness. In the second place, the words 'Voyagers' and 'seamen' direct the exhortation at those whose struggles and suffering were the subject of Movement II. The reader feels that a circuit is completed as the thought moves from acute personal distress, at the beginning of Movement II, through various stages of reflection and generalization, back to the personal situation, having gathered a word of wisdom on the way. In particular another answer is here given to the question asked in the fourth stanza of the lyric:

> 'Where is the end of them, the fishermen sailing
> Into the wind's tail, where the fog cowers?'

(DS 67–8)

with its complaint that we cannot think of a future

> 'that is not liable
> Like the past to have no destination.'
>
> (DS 71–2)

The 'real destination' here promised is not a local destination, for Eliot uses the word in its less usual sense, 'the end or purpose for which a person or thing is destined' (see *Oxford Dictionary*). Thus the 'real destination' is the same whether one comes to port or suffers 'the trial and judgement of the sea'. It is to achieve detachment, faring disinterestedly forward without the selfish concern to 'fare well'.

IV

Lady, whose shrine stands on the promontory

This lyric is rich in symbolic overtones. Some of them, however, are delicately sounded and the mere business of identifying them is apt to irritate because of the exaggeration inevitable in giving them the status of the articulate. With this proviso one may note that the Virgin Mary's central role in a poem whose subject is the need for obedient submission before the great annunciations which impose costly demands upon men and women is obvious and appropriate; but the filling out of this role so as to give it the maximum richness and universality while yet avoiding the temptation to versify dogmatic propaganda tests the poet sharply. Few people would deny that Eliot's magnificence depends greatly on the poetic skill which he brought to the resolution of this problem.

That the Virgin's shrine 'stands on the promontory' carries rich overtones. It reminds us that the Virgin's place (historic and philosophic) is at the point where the land, whose soil is the nourishment and end of life in the flesh, juts out into the waters, whose nearer waves are the waves of time but whose farther reaches represent the sea of eternity.

In asking the Virgin to pray 'for all those who are in ships', the poet seems to be making a generalized plea for all suffering and struggling people (men especially: see next stanza), but the three following lines (*DS* 171–3) appear to hint at a systematic categorization of people. Those whose 'business has to do with fish' (*DS* 171) would seem to refer to the Church. The word 'fish' has previously carried something like the symbolic overtones it carries in Joyce's *Ulysses* (see *BN* 134, *DS* 19). The word 'business', here as earlier (*EC* 189), recalls our Lord's words on the need to be about his 'father's business' and also the psalmist's 'They that go down to the sea in ships and occupy their business in great waters . . .' (cf. *DS* 179). Those 'concerned with every lawful traffic' obviously constitute the world of commerce and industry; while those who 'conduct them' are presumably those who govern and administer. Thus the three estates of Church, Industry, and Government seem to be referred to.

Repeat a prayer also

The Virgin was addressed in the first stanza as our 'Lady', in her universal and historic capacity as the agent of the Incarnation standing at the central point of intersection of the timeless with time. Hence the appropriateness of the generalized prayers for all in their human and larger public capacities. In this stanza the Virgin is addressed as the Mater Dolorosa, the sorrowing Mother, daughter of her own Son, who is yet 'Queen of Heaven'. The prayer now is for women, who bear the suffering of bereavement as work or war deprives them of sons or husbands.

The conciseness and clarity of the naming of the Virgin, in a poem so characterized by unuttered words, resounds with a sudden mysterious profundity. The emphatic definition of the Virgin's paradoxical role, as the most human daughter of the divine Son and the Queen of Heaven, itself sharply elucidates the end and destination to which the poem's exploratory hints and guesses, sudden illuminations and discursive speculations, are all alike leading, and foreshadows the coming utterance of the word 'Incarnation' in the next movement (*DS* 215). Moreover, the use of Dante's phrase, 'Figlia del tuo figlio' (*DS* 177), by its directness and explicitness, injects into the poem a concentrated infusion of allusive overtones of a kind which oblique and less readily identifiable literary echoes establish only gradually. The technical point is important because the distinction between a diluted and a concentrated infusion of poetic correspondence is parallel to the distinction between the fitful, particular, experiential hints of an eternal intersecting a temporal order, and the decisive archetypal act of divine Incarnation of which the Virgin Mary is the instrument. What is hinted at in man's intermittent glimpses of the eternal, the sudden shafts of sunlight momentarily transfiguring the world, is rendered fully articulate in the incarnation of God in man. Similarly, we may say, what is hinted at in every poetic citation of time momentarily transcended by a glimpse of beauty or of love is rendered fully articulate at the poetic level in Dante's full-scale exploration of the Affirmative Way, when christianly understood, and as elucidated by Charles Williams, for whose work Eliot always had an immense enthusiasm.

In the corresponding movements of *East Coker* and *Little Gidding* we arrive at Christ and at the Holy Spirit, the redeeming crucified Saviour and the descending Dove, as the divine Agents of recovery and restoration through suffering and through fire (still operating institutionally in mass and absolution, through sacrament and apostolic succession). In this movement the figure of the Virgin Mary is before us as the one whose Annunciation is the pattern of all human vocations to self-sacrifice, whose obedient response should be the pattern of all human responses to vocational demands. She is also by implication the archetypal representative of all that is affirmatively granted in the experience of love, beauty, and creativity. Because she is Dante's Virgin she introduces decisively into the poem the doctrine of the Beatrician Way, the theology of love with which those who share Eliot's enthusiasm for Charles Williams will be familiar (see *The Figure of Beatrice* and *He Came Down from Heaven*).

In this connection it should be noted that St Bernard's prayer for Dante the poet when, like the poet of *The Dry Salvages*, he has reached the point of maximum need and supplication, as it begins with the line here quoted, *Vergine madre, figlia del tuo figlio*, soon moves to the significant image –

> 'Nel ventre tuo si raccese l'amore
> per lo cui caldo nell' eterna pace
> così è germinato questo fiore.'
>
> (*Par.* XXXIII, 7–9.)

> (Within your womb the love was made to burn again, by whose warmth in the eternal peace this flower has bloomed.)

The dominance of the Virgin in *The Dry Salvages* thus throws back upon the unfolding flower of the *Burnt Norton* garden the associations of a Virgin-born Divinity, and further enriches the central incarnational significance of the symbolic rose. (It must be understood that in thus elaborating the lyrical prayer to the Virgin we rely not only on what the poet has already said, but on what he has yet to say, notably in *DS* V and *LG* V.)

Also pray for those who were in ships

The final prayer is for those who have come to a disastrous end by accident or violence, in peace or war, whether on shore, or sea's edge, or out in the deep. The date of composition makes it likely that wartime deaths of sailors and airmen are especially in mind, but in view of what follows, the wartime reference must not be regarded as exclusive. For here perhaps we first suspect that those 'on the deck of the drumming liner' (*DS* 142), warned not to think of a future before them, may be on a doomed vessel. Thus the night voice 'in the rigging and the aerial' (*DS* 146) which speaks 'not to the ear' and 'not in any language' (*DS* 147–8), is also a radio S.O.S. in morse. For identification of the vessel as the *Titanic* see App. III, 4.

The correspondence between the fourth movements of *East Coker*, *The Dry Salvages*, and *Little Gidding* is now unmistakable. The three lyrics speak of Christ, the Virgin Mary, and the Holy Spirit respectively. As *East Coker* IV ends with the image of the sacramental food and drink, the body and blood of Christ, broken and shed on Good Friday, so *The Dry Salvages* IV ends here with the sound of the perpetual *Angelus*, and the two ceremonies in which points of intersection of the timeless with time are institutionally recorded themselves provide instances of that practice of 'recovery' which Eliot seems to recommend equally in the spheres of poetic composition and of religious life. Eliot's achievement of a harmonious blend in his cultural and religious thought and practice must be noted whether or not one can sympathize with his views.

The endings of Movements I and IV of this Quartet, considered together

> 'Clangs
> The bell' (*DS* 47–8)

and

> 'the sea bell's
> Perpetual Angelus' (*DS* 182–3)

strangely recall

> 'the tolling bell's perpetual clang'

of Walt Whitman's threnody on the death of Lincoln, *When lilacs last in the dooryard bloomed* (already echoed in *DS* 12). The fact that the poet (Whitman) listens in this poem to the song of the thrush (who sings a song to Death) and that he emphasizes death's healing power over the combatants in the Civil War makes Eliot's echo a notable one.

The allusiveness of the imagery in this lyric gradually extends the range of reference. By imposing on obvious contemporary references to deaths in the Second World War (*DS* 180–1) the memory of the American Civil War, Eliot has once more peopled his poem, this time especially with a vast concourse of suffering women who have shared the agony of the Virgin Mary in the loss of their menfolk. The phrase

> 'who have seen their sons and husbands
> Setting forth' (*DS* 175–6)

echoes Donne's *Good Friday, Riding Westward,*

> 'There I should see a Sun by rising set
> And by that setting endless day beget.'

The association is a rich one, packed with relevance. Sharing in the suffering of others has brought us, as readers, into the company of the Virgin Mary who is waiting at the foot of the Cross till the black cloud carries her Son away (see *BN* 128): but that is only half the story, as the quotation from Donne implies. By that 'setting' of the Sun 'endless day' is begotten, so the cloud which carries away both the Son and the sun (at nightfall) will no more have power to 'bury the day' (or the Dayspring) of *BN* 127. (After the multifarious exploitations of the word 'end', readers may well consider that 'endless day' is a rich addition to the unspoken words of *Four Quartets*.) The Virgin into whose company we have come is not only the sorrowing Mother, she is also the Queen of Heaven (*DS* 178) in the garden of whose womb the eternal flower was made to bloom, and who grants to the suppliant poet the brief glimpse of the Beatific Vision. Perhaps we can now fully understand why Eliot introduced into *Burnt Norton* I an echo of *Andrea del Sarto* (36). Andrea too watches the sun set, as 'autumn grows, autumn in everything', and listens to the chapel bell, dreaming of the might-have-been past and of the 'Four great walls in the New Jerusalem', and staring at the city of Florence. And it is the painter Andrea's Virgin 'who is his wife'. The Joycean complexity of the network of allusions and cross-references (involving Dante, Donne, and Browning) is a revealing instance of Eliot's poetic method at this stage. The total effect of its emergence at this point of the poem is to throw backward upon the garden revelation of *Burnt Norton* I and forward upon the concluding vision of *Little Gidding* V glimpses of the transfigured City from *Revelations* in the form of the mystical Bride adorned for her Royal Spouse.

V

To communicate with Mars, converse with spirits

At the beginning of the last movements of the other three *Quartets* Eliot is concerned with the search for meaning and pattern in art, music, literature (the organization of words), and poetry especially. In each case the poet recognizes that the pattern established by the artist is a valid expression of the way in which pattern and meaning can be derived from experience of life. Indeed the poet's work in garnering the harvest of revelatory moments in his own life, seeing their supra-temporal inter-relatedness, first with what precedes and what succeeds them in his own personal experience, and then with the gathered intensities, the past- and future-packed 'presents' of former poets' lives – as figured and alive in their own masterpieces – is an instance of that process of self-transcending 'recovery' by which all life, alike at the personal, religious, cultural, and historical levels, can be rendered truly 'fruitful'.

Here, in the last movement of *The Dry Salvages*, Eliot turns first to pass judgement on other, and fruitless, ways of seeking for meaning. He lists a series of studies and practices in which people try to escape the limitations of the immediate present by reading the future and the past or otherwise extending their range of knowledge at the level of satisfying 'curiosity'. The apparent mingling of some genuinely scientific pursuits with pseudo-scientific explorations of the paranormal and with crude superstitious practices is remarkable at first sight. Research into the question whether there is life on other planets ('To communicate with Mars', *DS* 184) and post-Freudian psycho-analytic explorations of the subconscious (*DS* 192–4) are listed alongside references to spiritualist seances ('converse with spirits'), the casting of horoscopes, the study of entrails ('haruspicate'), and crystal-gazing ('scry'), as well as the reading of hand-writing, playing-cards, palms, and tea-leaves. It seems to be implied that divination by lottery ('sortilege'), astrology, necromancy (fiddling with penta-grams), drug-taking (fiddling with barbituric acids), and even the emphatically archaic process of reporting 'the behaviour of the sea monster' (DS 185) are on a level with psychological elucidation of the racial consciousness and subconsciousness with their archetypal images and hidden fears.

In view of this vein of apparent incongruity one is entitled to ask whether Eliot is doing anything more than having a good-humoured dig at the psychologists. Eliot's sense of humour, an important and neglected element in his work, is always to be reckoned with and is certainly evident here; but he does not indulge it at the expense of reason or fitness. A telling point is made. The practices and studies listed are all attempts to probe past and future, to escape the present or the normal without proper recognition of the 'timeless'. In the paranormal and superstitious practices referred to there is an attempt to achieve a supra-temporal view, but because it is mentally acquisitive, rooted in grasping 'curiosity', and devoid of open receptiveness to what is given in the reve-latory moments of personal experiences and that garnered harvest of revelatory experience which we call tradition (literary and religious), the attempt achieves only a spurious supra-temporality. The acquisitive grasp at past or future only serves to establish the self more firmly in its servitude to successiveness.

> 'Men's curiosity searches past and future
> And clings to that dimension' (DS 199–200).

The posture and motive belonging to popular explora-tion of the paranormal and the preternatural, being essenti-ally selfish and time-locked, are to be firmly distinguished from the posture and motive belonging to that disciplined openness to the supernatural which the poet's faith and experience present to him as the true way. It is, of course, the way of the saint.

Eliot pinpoints with great exactness three aspects of the attempts to arrive at meaning and understanding while firmly enchained to successiveness by describing these attempts as 'pastimes and drugs, and features of the press' (*DS* 195). The word 'pastimes' emphasizes both that they are trivial and that they do not free man from his time-locked status but merely help to whisk him meaninglessly along the stream of time. The word 'drugs' emphasizes both that the attempts are unhealthy (and, in the deepest sense, unnatural) and that they do not open man's mind to fuller insight but close it in a state of wasteful stupor. The word 'features' emphasizes both that they are emptily sensational and that they do not truly nourish the mind (as facts would do or even as worth-while imaginative fiction might do) but titillate it with the kind of snippetty, indisciplined journalistic informativeness which impoverishes thought.

A passage from St Luke's Gospel is decisively echoed in line 197.

> 'And there shall be signs in the sun and in the moon, and in the stars; and upon earth distress of nations with perplexity; the sea and the waves roaring: Men's hearts failing them for fear, and for looking after those things which are coming on earth: for the powers of heaven shall be shaken'.
>
> (St Luke XXI, 25–6)

This passage foretells the Second Coming of Christ. It is at times of unsettlement especially that men have recourse to the dabblers in superstition, witchcraft, black-magic, and even psycho-analysis. The poet lightly links such phases of modern unsettlement with the disturbances biblically prophesied to herald the Second Coming so as to match the half-fear of an end to all things hinted at in the earlier image of darkness between the acts in *East Coker* (115 ff.).

Over against the servitude to successiveness, Eliot defines the way of sanctity. The passage is finely compact and lucid. Indeed lines 199–215 might justly be said to provide the neatest and meatiest summary of the poem's central message, were it not that the poem is so carefully designed to discourage critics from using words like *message*. At least one may say that the lines formulate propositions and images in such a way as to provide an anchorage from which the reader may steadily and reliably explore the whole poem. It is scarcely possible to speak intelligently about *Four Quartets* without quoting the lines:

> 'But to apprehend
> The point of intersection of the timeless
> With time, is an occupation for the saint –'

since, as we have shown, those points of intersection are the starting-points of experience and reflection and (if we may be excused for using words as Eliot's own practice encourages us to use them) they point, each of them, to that central 'still point' (*BN* 62) at the heart of the turning world. They 'point to one end which is always present' (*BN* 10). They 'point to the agony of death and birth' (*EC* 132). And they are to be distinguished from the natural successiveness by which 'dawn points' (*EC* 47) compulsively to 'another day' just like the last one. The full apprehension of these points 'is an occupation for the saint' (*DS* 202), Eliot says; then he immediately cancels out the statement with –

> 'No occupation either, but something given
> And taken . . .' (*DS* 203–4).

It is plain that the first use of the word 'occupation' is the usual one. The apprehension of the point of intersection is something which will occupy the saint – keep him busy and, indeed, be his business (the double connotation is important). But it is not an 'occupation' in the professional sense: one cannot thereby earn a living: nor is it an 'occupation' in the sense that a person occupies a house or a position.

There is no rightful possession, no *occupancy*, no established footing as it were. On the contrary there is only the lifelong discipline of ardent self-surrender. What happens is that something is freely 'given' and humbly 'taken'.

Though the giving and the taking form the basis of a lifetime's disciplined service if one pursues vocationally the way of sanctity, there is for 'most of us' only the 'unattended moment', the sudden revelation, occasionally fully savoured, but more often half-glimpsed, by which we are jerked out of our habitual enslavement to time. Eliot repeats again the familiar images which instance the glimpse or the half-glimpse of illumination from 'out of time'. That they have a personal autobiographical base is not to be doubted; but the base is literary as well as directly experiential, for so the reiteration of the Shakespearean 'wild thyme' indicates. In the same way the 'waterfall' probably derives from Longfellow's *Hiawatha*.* The music 'heard so deeply/That it is not heard at all', which takes us back to the paradisal garden of *Burnt Norton* (27) somehow persistently recalls Keats's 'Heard melodies are sweet, but those unheard/Are sweeter' (*Ode on a Grecian Urn*), while 'you are the music/While the music lasts' has a faint Shelleyan ring. It seems likely that Eliot's conscious intention was to produce precisely this sense of moments personally authentic yet rich with the echoes of other men's comparable experiences. Such an intention would be in keeping with all that the poem has to say.

Recognizing and interpreting the revelatory moments as hints and glimpses of the meaning and the mystery lying behind our temporal framework is only one part of the Christian way: the other and complementary part is practising the traditional disciplines of prayer and worship, integrated with congruous study and behaviour. The unifying principle, the unifying word (Word), the unifying fact, historic and personal, is 'Incarnation' (*DS* 215). As God's

* On *Hiawatha*, see p. 182 and Appendix II. And see the comment on Tennysonian echoes (pp. 49–50).

incarnation in Christ (the timeless intersecting time) gave flesh and blood to the eternal, so the individual's life of self-surrender in the patterned Christian way is itself incarnational. It is important to notice the balance in line 215. The 'hint half guessed' is the revelatory moment: the 'gift half understood', taking us back to 'something given/And taken . . .' (DS 203-4), is the saint's 'occupation', the life of discipline, a gift because it is achieved only by grace. So every revelatory experience is an annunciation: it is also, like every Christian life, an incarnation. Christ's earthly career, the 'lifetime's death in love' (DS 204), is the archetypal Incarnation from which all other incarnations derive their validity.

Here the impossible union

'Here' means 'in the fact of Incarnation' as well as 'in the here and now': that is to say, in the incarnate life of Christ, and likewise in the individual Christian's recognition and practice of incarnation. The union of the two 'spheres of existence' (DS 217), eternal and finite, timeless and temporal, is actualized in the life of Christ at the archetypal level. The same union is actualized in every revelatory moment, properly understood, as gathering together past and future in a present illumination. Likewise the same union is actualized in every life of Christian discipline, every 'lifetime's death in love' (DS 204) – indeed in every act of 'ardour and selflessness and self-surrender' (DS 205), for each such act is an act enabled by grace, something 'given and taken', not something done from a motivating impulse within the line of temporal successiveness, not something done out of acquisitive desire directed at the future, but something done by *being 'moved'* (DS 221), divinely moved. The antithesis here is crucial. It is deeply interwoven in the whole Eliot canon.

Action under the dominance of the incarnational principle, by acceptance of the interpenetration of the timeless into time, is freed from that enchainment to temporal successiveness by which the world moves 'in appetency' (BN 125).

Such action is, in one sense, not action at all, but rather
patience (i.e. being acted upon) and *suffering*. For it involves
accepting that, morally and spiritually, man has 'no source of
movement' (*DS* 222) in himself. Time-locked action based
on servitude to the future is an attempt at movement on the
part of an agent, the human will,

> 'which is only moved
> And has in it no source of movement' (*DS* 221-2).

Man's moral will is moved either by the divinely incarnational principle on the one hand, or by 'demonic, chthonic/
Powers' (*DS* 223-4) on the other hand. Thus

> 'right action is freedom
> From past and future also' (*DS* 224-5).

It is freedom from servitude to time. It is the act not of an
actor but of a *patient*. The image of the whole earth as a
hospital (*EC* 157 ff.) is the logical outcome of this train of
thought whose roots lie back in *Murder in the Cathedral* –

> 'They know and do not know, what it is to act or suffer.
> They know and do not know, that acting is suffering
> And suffering is action. Neither does the actor suffer
> Nor the patient act. But both are fixed
> In an eternal action, an eternal patience
> To which all must consent that it may be willed
> And which all must suffer that they may will it,
> That the pattern may subsist, for the pattern is the action
> And the suffering, that the wheel may turn and still
> Be for ever still.'

After the high definition of the incarnational vocation, the
poet grants that 'for most of us' the aim is one which we
shall not realize 'here'. (The 'here' suggests that it will be for
us to realize it hereafter nevertheless.) We do not succeed.
We are undefeated only in the sense that we have not given
in but have 'gone on trying'. Thus the third *Quartet* ends on
a delightfully sympathetic and indulgent note which offsets
the rigours of its earlier definitions with an appropriate and

humble concession to the natural man in all his unassuming yet lovable weakness. For this I take to be the note of the last four lines. As natural men we revert to the earth which bred us, naturally and unexaltedly content to think that, as our temporal course ends and the cycle of life in the flesh is fully rounded off, what remains of us will enrich the nourishing soil. This is our expectancy as unregenerate men who have set our sights too low to achieve the way of sanctity; this is the inheritance we look for as men unheroic in the ways of the spirit – that we should return to the earth, to rest, having made more meaningful the life of earth. Our modest aim as spiritual beings, but half awake to the costly and lofty religious calling, can be parenthetically summed up in the concession that we hope to lie 'not too far from the yew-tree' – not too far from the shelter of that tree which we are not even bold enough (or certain enough) to call a cross.

Little Gidding

I

Midwinter spring is its own season

The Huntingdonshire village of Little Gidding, the starting-point of the fourth poem, is significant on several counts. Here Nicholas Ferrar settled in 1625, having abandoned a promising career, first in scholarship, as a Fellow of Clare Hall, Cambridge, later in business as Deputy-Treasurer of the Virginia Company. He was ordained deacon by Laud, came to Little Gidding, gathered relations around him and established a community in which the religious disciplines of regular offices and vigils were combined with active works of charity among the poor and the sick, with teaching, study, and the practice of crafts. It is known that George Herbert visited the house; Charles I called in 1633, and perhaps stayed there overnight after his defeat at Naseby in 1645. Cromwell's men later raided the community, which was broken up in 1647.

Little Gidding stands as a symbol of reconciliation. The community's unique blend of religious discipline and family life makes the place a peculiarly powerful symbol of reconciliation between the way of Negation and the way of Affirmation, between the practice of austerity and the acceptance of life's revelatory richness, the way of the fire and the way of the rose. The place is now also a symbol of past conflicts resolved – the conflict between King and Parliament, Episcopacy and Dissent, the Catholic and the Evangelical strains in Christian doctrine and practice. For all these reasons it is important to Eliot's thematic scheme.

We have noted that the might-have-been Paradise of ordered family life imaged in the *Burnt Norton* garden was representative of childhood innocence as of the innocence of man in the Garden of Eden before the Fall. It becomes also, by virtue of certain overtones and links later in this last poem (see especially *LG* 175–6), representative of the might-have-been pattern of historic harmony and unity which events such as the Civil War and the emigration of Eliots and their like disturbed. Obviously the parallelism here must not be pushed too far or read too mechanically; but the fact of Eliot's return from St Louis to Massachusetts, to England, and especially to East Coker and Little Gidding, must be seen in relation to his 'recovery' of the past as poet, as citizen, as Christian. The poet went back to feed on the work of seventeenth-century forbears and on the central tradition of European poetry; the American adopted British nationality; the citizen of a Republic became a monarchist; the Christian bred of a Congregationalist family became an Anglican High Churchman. These 'returns' ('Return, Thomas, return!') have – for poetic purposes – what can only be called a penitential aspect. For this reason it is interesting that before long we shall find reason to suspect that Eliot is faintly but deliberately echoing the story of the Prodigal Son (*LG* 29–31: see pp. 128, 151, and 153).

In the elemental scheme *Little Gidding* is concerned with Fire, where *Burnt Norton* was concerned with Air, *East Coker* with Earth, and *The Dry Salvages* with Water. In the theological scheme fire is associated with the pentecostal tongues of flame which hung over the heads of the apostles at the coming of the Holy Ghost, and whose apostolic significance and symbolism are still preserved in the episcopal mitre. (This point is noteworthy in view of Charles I's connection with the defence of episcopacy and of Eliot's attachment alike to seventeenth-century and to twentieth-century Anglican Catholicism.) Fire is also associated with the purifying flames of purgatorial discipline, with the burning power of Divine Love, and with the ardour of human passion. The rich variety of the fire symbolism in a poem part of whose background is the burning London of the wartime blitz is potent and far-reaching.

'Midwinter spring', with its reconciliation of frost and fire, is the appropriate time for a visit to Little Gidding. The day of sunshine in the middle of winter has various symbolic significances. It is a season of its own that breaks the natural cycle. Its shaft of sunlight is a point of illumination intersecting time's familiar routine of successiveness. It belongs, in a sense therefore, to the pattern of the timeless. Hence it is 'sempiternal' (*LG* 2). The word 'sodden' (*LG* 2) takes us back to *BN* 58 and thereby hints perhaps at the renewal of the personal rapture of *BN* II (49 ff.) in the winter of age. The ambiguous phrase, 'suspended in time' (the unnatural season *hanging* like an incursion into time, and also suddenly *broken off*), reinforces too the notion of a suspension of the natural sequence of the seasonal round, and the phrase, 'between pole and tropic', further presses the momentary paradoxical reconciliation of extremes. As the paradoxical images accumulate – frost and fire, flames on ice, cold that warms the heart – the mind inevitably goes back especially to lines 162–6 of *East Coker*. There the imagery (cf. 'frigid purgatorial fires') pointed to the painful disciplinary aspect of the fire-frost paradox. Here the emphasis is upon its joyful aspect: the intense glow 'Stirs the dumb spirit' (*LG* 10), for the fire is no longer purgatorial but pentecostal; not punitive, retributive, or disciplinary, but a gift of the Holy Spirit 'in the dark time of the year'. The blinding 'glare' that is reflected in a watery mirror (*LG* 7–8) decisively brings back the first seminal revelatory experience in the paradisal garden (*BN* 35). Thus Eliot shows again how the negative and affirmative aspects of the Christian way represent two balancing complementary statements of a single truth. The relationship of this reconciliation with what has gone before is further pressed in the lines,

> 'Between melting and freezing
> The soul's sap quivers.'
> (*LG* 11–12)

which recall on the one hand the affirmative dance of blood and the ascent of sap in the earlier experience of reconciliation

(*BN* 49–56) – the phrase 'sap quivers' brilliantly draws together the movement of sap in the tree and the image of the 'trilling wire in the blood' – and on the other hand the negative ascent of chill and feverous singing in 'mental wires' in the freezing purgatory imaged in the hospital stanzas of *East Coker* IV (162–5).

The lack of 'earth smell' or 'smell of living thing' (*LG* 12–13) – smells which are pungent in *East Coker* I – again differentiates this springtime, which is not in the covenant guaranteed by time's natural cycle, from the time-bound summer of *East Coker* I, subject to decay, savouring of dung and death. The white that blossoms here is the white of snow on the hedgerow, bright in the midday sun. The blossom is 'transitory', not in the sense that it buds and fades with the movement of the seasonal cycle, but that it is suddenly given (*LG* 16) and equally suddenly taken away (see above, line 3, 'suspended in time'). It is not part of the 'scheme of generation' (*LG* 18) of plant and men so fully explicated in *East Coker* I. Here is a spring from outside time, and one must not look for a summer within time to follow it. Indeed the appropriate 'summer' to follow this spring would be a 'Zero summer' (*LG* 20), a summer paradoxically produced by a winter whose wintriness had reached the bottom of the temperature chart. (The faint indirect echo of the *East Coker* 'fever chart', *EC* 151, in this use of the word 'Zero' is apt.) But such a summer is 'unimaginable'. Not thus, not within time's covenant, will the 'enigma' be resolved. (Cf. *EC* 151.)

Looking back at the end of this section, one is struck by the series of phrases ('between pole and tropic', *LG* 3, 'Between melting and freezing', *LG* 11, and 'neither budding nor fading', *LG* 17) which together establish, as a starting-point for the last *Quartet*, what might be called a position *between* positions, or (to move from local to temporal metaphor) an interval between times. The poet wrestles with language in the attempt, not to plant the reader here or there, but rather to *unplant* him, to lift him wholly out of the world of successiveness with all its familiarities – natural, geographical, and climatic. We may recall that it was during an interval of non-expectancy that the vision was first granted in *Burnt Norton* I. One can have 'no occupation' (*DS* 203) when the 'occupation for the saint' (*DS* 202) is about to be given and taken. The temporal displacement of the reader is at first a de-positioning of the body – that is of the senses, whose familiar world of warmth or cold (*LG* 11), scent and savour (*LG* 11–12), growth and fading (*LG* 17) is suddenly taken away. The importance of here uprooting the reader (a process that is even more evident in *LG* 78 ff.) is that it prepares him for the descent of the Dove of *LG* IV, for the 'one discharge' (*LG* 203) of fire and flame which must be experienced before he is ready for the final vision of *Little Gidding* V. (And see App. III, 5.)

If you came this way

The conditional clauses perform an important function here. We move from various hypothetical positions to the actual location, Little Gidding. This movement reverses what happened in the opening of *Burnt Norton*. There we moved from the actual to the hypothetical – the might-have-been garden. The movement proved also to be from the temporal to the eternal. Here we move from the hypothetical to the actual – to discover that our location 'in place and time' (*LG* 38) can once again induce 'the intersection of the timeless moment' (*LG* 52).

The first hypothesis – if you came from the most probable (but undefined) place by the most probable (but undefined) route – deposits you here against a natural background which, unlike the background of the last section, is firmly located in the normal seasonal round. It is the genuine 'maytime' of real May, not now 'midwinter spring'. The hedges are white with real blossom, not with snow which looks blossomlike. The deeper meaning of the contrast is pressed upon us in the phrase 'voluptuary sweetness' (*LG* 24). The chaste, spiritualized loveliness of the sudden bloom in midwinter spring was well caught by the word 'blanched' (*LG* 15), but the white beauty of the actual may-blossom, as it has the added sensuous richness, so too it has the added taint of that which might too dangerously and seductively allure. All this is sharply hinted at in the words 'voluptuary sweetness'.

Whoever you are and from wherever you came, at whatever time and from whatever motive (if any at all), the actual place arrived at would be the same. You come face to face with 'the dull façade/And the tombstone' (*LG* 29–30), with the fact that our imposing civilization is a transitory, insubstantial one (for the 'façade' takes us back to that 'imposing' scenic façade of *EC* 117 which we know is to be 'rolled away') and with the fact of death. This is what confronts all who fully face the actual. It was what faced Charles I, the 'broken king', when and if he came here after his defeat at Naseby. It is what faces the casual, motiveless visitor.

The poet himself, we have said, comes in a penitential mood. There are faint verbal echoes here which suggest that the return of the Prodigal Son was in Eliot's mind. It must be admitted that, in the case of a poet like Eliot whose allusiveness is constant yet often subtle and delicate, one cannot always distinguish between effects intentionally contrived and those produced by sheer coincidence. This said, we may note that the emphatic word 'journey' in line 25 (recalling also Eliot's Magi – other 'broken' kings) and the reference to the 'pig-sty' in close proximity to the notable word 'husk' (*LG* 29 and 31) together constitute a little verbal cluster that is reminiscent of St Luke XV (see 11–32) for anyone who generally recognizes how much Biblical echoing there is in Eliot, and more particularly senses the aptness of reference to a parable in which the Father welcomes the returned erring son back to 'musick and dancing' and strives to reconcile wandering brother with stay-at-home brother at the same celebration. (Later evidence strengthens this reading. See p. 153.)

Real 'ends' (purposes) are once more distinguished from

superficial temporal motives in lines 30–5. The meaning
of an act is not the same as the motive which you may have
read into it in advance. The motive that may have brought
you to Little Gidding is but the 'shell' in which the true purpose is contained (and that was why it was not worth bother-
ing to define this motive exactly above, *LG* 21–3: any
hypothetical motive would serve). The true purpose will
emerge only when the 'shell' has been broken, and the
insubstantiality of the assumed motive thereby made plain.
There is a notable ambiguity in the phrase 'only when it is
fulfilled' (*LG* 32). We may paraphrase: (i) 'The true purpose
emerges only when it (the purpose) is fulfilled (realized)', and
(ii) 'The true purpose emerges only when it (the shell – the
superficial motive) is full-filled with meaning and therefore
cracks under the pressure of the new and living content.'
The packed thought here is universally relevant. What Eliot
has to say about the relationship between motive and meaning, or purpose, is a crucial part of the elaborate, tightly-
knit web of moral, intellectual, and spiritual insights which
constitutes Eliot's reading of the human situation. Thus he
limits further the significance of conscious human motivation at the purely temporal level in lines 33–5. Whether you
act with a purpose (an end) in mind or with no purpose in
mind, the true purpose is something beyond what can be
anticipated in advance and different from it. The 'fulfilment'
– the filling full of the supposed 'end' (original, *a priori*
temporal motive) with meaning which bursts out, and the
realization of significance which emerges in experience –
cannot be 'figured' in advance because, as was said in *EC*
85–7,

> 'the pattern is new in every moment
> And every moment is a new and shocking
> Valuation of all we have been.'

Humility, we learned also in *East Coker*, is 'endless' in two
senses. It does not pursue its own ends: nor does faith: nor
does hope, properly understood. All this is implicit in the

doctrine of Grace and eminently relevant in a Quartet whose central figure is the Holy Spirit.

Man comes up against his true end when the 'dull façade/ And the tombstone' confront him. There are many 'other places' at which man may come to the 'world's end' (and once more the end of the world is connoted as well as the end of man's life). The locations of violent wartime deaths are again listed: all bring their daily reminders of mortality to us. But at this moment of the poet's experience directly, and of the reader's experience indirectly, Little Gidding supplies the 'nearest' (*LG* 38) indication of what the 'world's end' is (the world's purpose as well as the world's transitoriness).

Thus, although we may now be said to have reached an actual place, what confronts us indicates that we have as yet (metaphorically to anticipate what is to follow) no *ground* to stand on. The extra-temporal physical suspension (of *LG* 1–20) is now matched with an extra-purposive mental suspension. The phrase 'husk of meaning' (*LG* 31) recalls 'empty of meaning' (*BN* 102), and indeed the prevalent sense of emptiness, physical and mental, created by the imagery of *LG* 30–5 is highly significant. In the first place we must recall the empty, drained pool of *BN* 33–4, which was soon to be filled with reflected light as the Spirit of God moved over it. Moreover, the empty concrete pool has already been obliquely associated with the emptying of the personality in disciplined preparation for the mystical experience (*BN* 117–21). In the second place the theme of emptiness hereabouts articulated in proximity to the word 'tombstone' (*LG* 30), to the suggestive phrase, 'broken king' (*LG* 26), as well as to the emphatic recall of the sunset– Sonset theme in *LG* 2, ('towards sundown') introduces the unspoken concept of the empty tomb. There can be no questioning of Eliot's intention here if we listen carefully to his music. The 'dull façade/And the tombstone' seem to balance each other in confronting man with the combination of transitoriness and death: but they also offer an Either/Or of meaninglessness or new life, for 'façade' takes us back to the scenery of *EC* III –

'And the bold imposing façade are all being rolled away'
(*EC* 117)

and on the morning of the Resurrection the disciples found the tombstone in the garden 'rolled away'. The unheard music, the unspoken word – if we follow the echoes till we find them – bring the rolled-away tombstone and the distant sound of angelic wings (*EC* 115) decisively into the mind in *LG* 30. (Rolled away façade or rolled away tombstone?)

What now confronts the reader of *Four Quartets* is a harmony of overtones clearly linking the unspoken concept of the empty tomb with both the empty pool and the emptied mind. Needless to say, the associations of the empty tomb in the garden of the Resurrection give the empty pool in the paradisal garden of *Burnt Norton* richer connotations as the window upon the eternal City. The full appropriateness of the clustering here (in *LG* I) of themes of emptiness along-side the theme of temporal and local displacement (more plainly articulated in *LG* 78 ff.) will emerge later – that is, if we read ourselves into acceptance of the principles enunciated in *LG* 30–5; for they apply to us as readers of *Little Gidding*, just as they would apply to us as visitors to Little Gidding. 'There are other places. . . . But this is the nearest' (*LG* 35 and 38).

If you came this way

We are invited to approach the village of Little Gidding a second time – and now the local and temporal starting-points are even vaguer. They are not defined even in terms of the probable (as at *LG* 21, 'Taking the route you would be likely to take') or even in terms of the hypothetical (as at *LG* 23–4, 'you would find the hedges/White again in May'). 'It would always be the same' (*LG* 28). The particular makes universally the same demand. The encounter with this actual place, charged with its own historic and present significance, makes the inescapable demand upon us that all points of intersection make – that we should 'put off/Sense and motion'. The emphatic line-end stress upon the words 'put off' carries biblical overtones. It leaves the reader half-expecting the next line to complete God's words to Moses. 'Put off thy shoes from off thy feet, for the place whereon thou standest is holy ground.' Exodus III, 5. This divine injunction is thematically in place; it comes from the midst of the *burning* bush, and Eliot has already defined the pentecostal fire as a 'glow more intense than blaze of branch' (*LG* 9). Thus the sudden blossoming of the hedge-row (*LG* 15) is now implicitly linked to the image of the burning bush, and the word 'covenant' ('not in time's covenant', *LG* 14) is re-charged with more precise *Old Testament* overtones. The elucidator may now add that even the phrase 'no wind' (*LG* 10), succeeding the words 'Stirs the dumb spirit', is rich in further hinted connections. The pentecostal fire in the *New Testament* came with a 'rushing mighty wind' (Acts II, 2), but *Little Gidding*'s symbol is fire 'in windless cold' (*LG* 6). The Lord was 'not in the wind' (I Kings XIX, 11) when the word came to the prophet Elijah, but in the still small voice. The hint which directs the mind to this encounter is surely intentional: for Elijah's complaint to the Lord in the context was that 'the children of Israel have forsaken Thy covenants, thrown down thine altars . . .' (I Kings XIX, 10) and Eliot too has later in mind the damaged and neglected 'sanctuary and choir' (*LG* 76).

Once more Eliot makes a clear distinction between the familiar conception of learning by experience natural to a secular, humanistic society, and the demand made by the holy ground, the burning bush, the sacred place of past dedication and present reconciliation. We are not asked knowingly 'to verify', assertively 'to instruct' ourselves, acquisitively 'to inform curiosity', self-importantly to 'carry report' (*LG* 43–5). (The word 'curiosity' has already been used with connotative emphasis on man's grasping, self-centred search for knowledge, *DS* 199, and the word 'report' likewise, *DS* 185.) It is noteworthy that we are not even asked 'to pray'; presumably because that would be to put the demand too actively – implying that we ourselves have a positive contribution to make by virtue of our own virtue. Rather we are simply asked 'to kneel/Where prayer has been valid'. The impersonal emphasis, lifting from us the load of personal assertiveness-in-righteousness, is important; for the very nature of true prayer itself, as here defined, calls for something simpler, humbler, more receptive, than consciously ordering words, giving the mind a job to do ('occupation of the praying mind'), and thus embarking on that complex, assertive activity in which there is a self, consciously praying, manipulating a vocabulary and hearing the performance of the voice. Prayer is none of these. There is no need to define what it is. Better merely to say that what the dead could not tell us when they were alive they can now tell us, being dead. The implication is that we must listen. But it is not an order, nor a recipe, for as such, put in the form of imperative or exhortation, the call to listen would reintroduce an invitation to the ego to assert itself in awarely listening. Thus the sentence, 'You are here to kneel/Where prayer has been valid', emerges as a concentrated non-exhortatory exploration at the existential level of what Kierkegaard says (*less* existentially!) in *Purity of Heart*.

What the dead have to tell us is 'tongued with fire' (*LG* 51). The phrase is charged with meaning from outside and from within the poem. The tongues of fire which descended on the Apostles' heads at Pentecost have remained symbolic of the Holy Spirit and of the apostolic authority of the Church: and the dead speak after having endured the flames of suffering and martyrdom. In short, the dead speak with the authority of the Spirit and from experience of the extremities of surrender and purgation. This is the utterance to which the poet listens in the silence of Little Gidding church and, later, in the dawn encounter with the 'compound ghost'. And the reader too, listening to Eliot himself, hears now the poet's communication, so little understood, during his lifetime. What the poet found at Little Gidding we can now find here, at *this*, our 'timeless moment', as it is intersected by the past which is Eliot's, King Charles's, anyone's; in England and yet anywhere and therefore *no where*; always and at any particular time and therefore at *no particular* time.

II

Ash on an old man's sleeve

This lyric explores the destructive power of the elements, air, earth, fire, and water. The emphasis is partly on the way one element disintegrates by contact with another. It is also, implicitly, on the ephemerality of what is contained within time. The conception of the cyclic transience of earthly existence, strong in *East Coker* I, is recreated: but this time one is made aware, not so much of man's servitude to the natural cycle ('Dung and death', *EC* 46), as of the insubstantiality of the living universe as a whole.

The first image seems to show an old man poking his garden bonfire, as the poet reminds us that, like the house timbers of *East Coker EC* 5, the roses of *Burnt Norton* end up as ash. Man's utterance too leaves a puff of dust in the air as he finishes speaking. This concept of a man coming to the end of his reminiscences would perhaps justify reading into line 54 the further image of an old man with tobacco ash on the fringe of his sleeve. Eliot is perhaps saying: Just as the rose-leaves in the garden finish up, after burning, as ash on the gardener's sleeve and a puff of dust in the air, so the rose-leaves of remembered joyful revelation finish up, after reminiscence, as ash on the talker's sleeve and a puff of dust in the air.

The puff of dust has now become a potent image. The *Quartets* began with the poet's finger poking into the bowl of our minds to disturb the dust on the rose-leaves of our memories. The fact that utterance of the word leaves a little

cloud of dust reminds us that utterance of the Word ended
in a cloud as the disciples looked up after the Ascension at
the ending of another story. We may remember too that
Eliot is much concerned in this Quartet with the scene in
blitz-ravaged London after an incendiary raid, when clouds
of dust marked the points of destruction where houses had
been hit.

In this connection, in order to do full justice to Eliot's
complex network of symbols, it may be helpful now to look
back not only to the crucial line,

'The black cloud carries the sun away' (*BN* 128),

with its sun/Son pun, relating man's involuntary death to
the ending of Christ's incarnate life, but also to the three
moments recorded in *Burnt Norton* 85–7; the moment 'in the
rose-garden', the moment 'in the arbour where the rain beat',
and the moment 'in the draughty church at smokefall', for
on each of these occasions it would appear that a cloud took
away the light. Perhaps we are now in a position to see
fuller significance in the cluster of these three moments at
that point in the poem; for it would appear that the last
moment, 'in the draughty church at smokefall' (*BN* 87) casts
forward both to the poet's particular visit to Little Gidding
church and to his generalized experience, recorded in *Little
Gidding*, of churches burnt out by air-raids. Thus new and
powerful correspondences can be detected between these
three *moments*. The first, by its connection with the Garden
of Eden, is associated with the Universal Fall of Man, who
has lost his paradisal innocence and happiness. The second
'moment' may be associated with a personal fall, to the
extent that, read in the light of later back-references, it
speaks of a taste of happiness given and taken, a paradise
glimpsed and lost. And the third 'moment', as we have
already explained, is associated with the Historic Fall by
which the human family's story has been one of internecine
strife.

Linking the various clouds and puffs of dust back to the

'black cloud' of *BN* 128, and so with the Crucifixion, is however, only half the 'story'. The reader who is thoroughly versed in the poem will also link these experiences of darkness forward to the crucial, emphatically isolated line which is to follow in *Little Gidding* 238,

'With the drawing of this Love and the voice of this Calling',

where we learn, if we attend to the reverberations of the *unspoken word*, that all our clouds are after all but fragments of the great Cloud of Unknowing and therefore – to use words which 'footfalls' of the Hound of Heaven recall –

'Shade of His hand, outstretched caressingly'.

The cloud is a shield, protecting us from the 'glare that is blindness in the early afternoon' (*LG* 8) and from the clarity of reflection which would reveal to us our chimera-like appearance (*BN* 158): it protects us from the 'heaven' which 'flesh cannot endure' (*BN* 82).

It will be evident from the course of our argument that, like *Cloud of Unknowing* (see *LG* 238), *Hound of Heaven* is an 'unspoken word' (cf. *Ash Wednesday* V) in *Four Quartets*. We arrive at it by following echoes ('footfalls') down a passage which Eliot did not take in the poem – the passage of direct utterance. It will be observed too that the unspoken words accumulate for the reader as he becomes more deeply immersed in *Four Quartets*: they include, for instance, the crucial names, God the Creator, Christ the Redeemer, the Virgin Mary, and the Holy Spirit. The wind is now shaking them as voices from the Yew-tree, as Eliot, in *Ash Wednesday* prophesied that it would. The reader is invited to attend to Eliot's subsequent exhortation –

'Let the other yew (*you*) be shaken and reply'.
(*Ash Wednesday* VI, 24.)

If we return now to the lyric before us, we shall find that its lines immediately throw us back again in mind, this time to *East Coker*, for the disintegration of a ruined house (*LG* 58 ff.), by which brick and stone and carved panelling are reduced to dust that is then breathed into human lungs, is as surely related to the poet's visit to East Coker (*EC* 2 and 12) as it is to the poet's experience of blitzed London. That the 'death of air' (*LG* 61) is 'the death of hope' is intelligible by virtue of Eliot's previous use of the word *hope* ('hope would be hope for the wrong thing', *EC* 124) as meaning attachment to terrestrial objects (and related aims), which are seen to end in dust. That the 'death of air' is also the 'death of despair' is a paradoxical converse. To get beyond the kind of hope which is rooted in the terrestrial is to escape from the concomitant despair which that kind of hope inevitably leads to. The fire which burns away the insubstantial substances in which one vainly trusts (whether it is a bonfire burning earth's dead roses, or a personal penitence and purgation burning one's past indulgences) lifts one above both hope and despair. We may recall that, in *Ash Wednesday*, the poet, striving to climb above his dead self, saw behind him the ghost of that dead self still

> 'Struggling with the devil of the stairs who wears
> The deceitful face of hope and of despair.'
> (*Ash Wednesday* III, 5–6)

There are flood and drouth

The first image bears the now-to-be-expected composite reference. The image of the corpse on the sea shore, the victim of water and earth, 'flood and drouth', is linked with other allusions in the poem to those who have met violent wartime deaths (cf. *DS* 180) but no doubt refers equally to one of the *personae* of the compound poet who left his 'body on a distant shore' (*LG* 125) – Shelley perhaps.* These instances should not be regarded as exclusive. Eliot's universality-in-particularity is as important as his particularity-in-universality. Death by water has been a persistent theme in Eliot's poetry, and Shakespeare's *Tempest* has had for him the capsulated symbolic usefulness that Joyce found

* For the possible allusive reference to Longfellow's *Hiawatha* here and elsewhere, see Appendix II.

in Milton's *Lycidas*. Sea and sand have both flooded and drained eyes and mouth in that combined process of salting, caking, and parching, which makes even death by water a thirsty death. That water and sand should be 'contending for the upper hand' means not only that sea and sand compete in the destructive work, but also, I take it, that one of the corpse's hands is so placed (in a small pool?) that some fingers are floating in water while others are covered in sand.

In the second half of the stanza we move from the sea-shore to the desert. Here the 'parched eviscerate soil' is devoid of the 'bone of man and beast' (*EC* 8), the decaying vegetable matter and the dung (*EC* 8 and 46) which made the soil of *East Coker* fruitful in the cyclic life of nature. The contrast with *East Coker* is pressed home. Here the utterly unfruitful soil shows up fully the long-term vanity of human labour. Its face presents us with a gaping, ironic laugh ('laughs without mirth' *LG* 68) at human effort, in sharp contrast with the 'rustic laughter' (*EC* 35) and the 'country mirth' (*EC* 37) of the generations of farming folk who lived off the soil of East Coker.

The parallels continually drawn between personal history, family history, national history, and racial history, and the continual shifting of focus and locale, have by this stage in one's experience of the poem fully established in the reader a habit of responding to the allusive abundance packed into the highly charged lyrical passages such as this. Thus one does not need to stretch the imagination far in order to sense behind the images of *LG* 66–9 an awareness of the disastrous cyclic effects, at the civilizational level, of exploiting the earth and its fruits, as exemplified in the dust-bowl* of the U.S.A. and even (if the Virgilian echoes and the echoes of the Second World War are borne in mind) the North African desert. The price paid for American and Roman prosperity and extravagance at a given stage of history is the mocking spectacle of dust-bowl and desert at another stage. This

* Note how the repeated 'Dust', 'Dust' of *LG* 56 and 58 reverberates with an echo of 'dust . . . bowl' from *BN* 16.

reflection, on the large-scale civilizational level, of the cyclic sequence explored on the level of family and village history in *East Coker* I and on the level of personal history for the man and the poet in *East Coker* II and V, is to receive its fullest articulation, in personal terms, later in this movement (*LG* 129 ff.).

Water and fire succeed

It is convenient to note the secondary meaning of the first line before the primary one. Water and fire *are successful*, where human labour, as we have just seen, is not. The poet traces backwards the cyclic development of civilization form a wartime angle. As the weed is succeeded by the pasture in the earliest stages of human agriculture and the pasture by the town in the later stages of civilization, so now the fire of the incendiary bomb destroys the town, and the water of the hoses puts out the fire. Eliot sees houses and churches burnt by bombs and then drenched by fire-fighters. This disastrous elemental rotation is at first sight in strong contrast to the slower and more civilized rotations of London life or of village life, of urban time (*BN* III) or of rural time (*EC* I). Nevertheless the cyclic pattern is common to all – to London workers plunging down into the earth for their journeys on the Underground and then coming back into the air (*BN* 108 ff.), to East Coker villagers lifting their 'earth feet' into the air (*EC* 36), then bringing them down to earth, and finally taking them under the earth (*EC* 38 and 100). The dance round the fire (*EC* 33), the rotation of the crops (*EC* 23), the successive rising and falling of feet and houses (*EC* 2), families and lineages (*EC* 9) – all these cyclic sequences are in mind as the poem moves to its most devastating presentations of human and elemental circuits finally self-consumed in fire.

The religious significance of water and fire is fully present to the mind too. The water of Baptism and the fire of the Holy Spirit themselves represent 'deaths' of another kind; for Baptism is death to sin and to the old unregenerate self, and the new life in the Spirit is both the burning away of selfishness in the fire which is purgation, and the heart's burning with love of God. The drenched and smoking ruins of a London church are clearly in the background as Eliot speaks of water and fire mocking our denial of the sacrificial Christian vocation and our neglect of the Church.

We have seen how the larger implications of the immediate lyrical presentation of a cyclic progress to the death of water and fire (a progress which is built into our experience on the personal, religious, historic, and natural planes), can be grasped by patient exploration of the poem as a whole. What the reader has to do is to accept the need for that repeated pursuit of thematic cross-references which the almost ritualistic recurrence of key words and images plainly demands of him. Although it is useful and stimulating to be familiar too with the technical philosophical background to the trains of thought followed here and elsewhere, it is far more important simply to appreciate the inter-relationships between section and section, theme and theme, figure and figure. With each successive movement it becomes clearer that the kind of reading required is parallel to the intense yet submissive mental alertness with which one listens to music, assimilating at one and the same time both the immediate figurative content, melodic and rhythmic, and the overall design to which it contributes and on which it is dependent for its force and relevance. The listener must be simultaneously sensitive to the immediate textural quality and to the total pattern which is woven of innumerable blends and contrasts cunningly phased over the work as a whole.

This said, it will be helpful to note the doctrine of Heraclitus to whose thought Eliot's own epigraph draws attention. Heraclitus's doctrine that everything is in a state of eternal flux because the elements themselves are involved in a cyclic sequence of mutual self-destruction, lies at the back of the presentation in this lyric as of some of the imagery of *East Coker* II. The theory of endless elemental conflict and material transmutation by which fire changes continually to water and then to earth, while earth changes continually back again to water and water to fire, in a repetitive downward, then upward, sequence, is plainly in the poet's mind.

Equally, of course, the doctrines of twentieth-century physics lie behind the lament at the apparently meaningless process of haphazardness and decay contained in *The Dry Salvages* II (e.g. *DS* 69 ff. and *DS* 80 ff.), and behind the picture of irresistible cyclic reversion to a final 'destructive fire' (*EC* 66) given us in *East Coker* 61–7. If the Heraclitan theory declares that the ultimate principle into which all existence is resolvable is fire, the Second Law of Thermodynamics foresees the final exhaustion of the energy available in our physical system and the consequent 'Heat-death' of the universe. The irreversible process of natural transformation, as seen by the modern physicist, involves increase of entropy and accompanying loss of energy, so that indeed ancient philosophy and modern science may be said to combine to substantiate the poet's reading of our human situation in terms of progress towards a death of fire (cf. *EC* 66 and *LG* 213). This 'substantiation', however, is but an intellectual back-cloth to the poet's imaginative exploration of the theme of fire. We do not need to examine the back-cloth in detail in order to understand and participate in what is being enacted in front of it. The enactment is an experiential probing of our own selves and of the situation in which those selves flourish and decay, live and die, or maybe – if they escape their servitude – die and live.

In the uncertain hour before the morning

The poet places us now at the time just before dawn which he has previously noted, in this poem and elsewhere, as a time of critical uncertainty:

'Between midnight and dawn, when the past is all deception,
 The future futureless, before the morning watch
 When time stops and time is never ending'

(*DS* 43–5).

Because, at this time, the night seems 'interminable' to those anxiously waiting for the day, the hour provides a fit symbolic background for the twentieth-century poet's encounter with his unidentified Master. A sentence in a recent review comes conveniently to hand to indicate the universal fascination for the twentieth-century writer of the critical time of expectancy –

> 'As the authors of *The Testament of Samuel Beckett* point out, his (Beckett's) work up to now has been an acknowledgment that we all live through a dubious Saturday, lit by fitful and instantly derided gleams of hope, between the Friday of the Crucifixion and the Sunday of the promised but scarcely believed in Resurrection.'
>
> (*Times Literary Supplement*, 30 June 1966)

One is repeatedly anticipating the end of what seems unending (and it may be added that this recurrency of expectation is itself the very *end*, that is purpose, of that which seems so intolerably endless – and purposeless).

The poet has been on night duty as a fire warden. The last bombers have gone, but the *All Clear* has not yet sounded. This situation reinforces the symbolic meaning of the hour located between night and day, between suffering and its sure expurgation, between destruction and restoration. The incendiary enemy dive-bomber, in a finely audacious paradoxical image, is related to the Holy Spirit, the dove which brings the tongue of flame, to purge by burning. This correspondence is in line with a long series of paradoxical images that constitute a decisive theme in Eliot's work. We may recall the powerful lines in *The Waste Land*,

> 'Oh keep the Dog far hence, that's friend to men,
> Or with his nails he'll dig it up again!' (74–5).

where Webster's 'foe' is changed to 'friend' and the capitalized 'Dog' is plainly 'God' spelt backwards. God, the Hound of Heaven, the friend who is the selfish self's loving enemy, will dig up the buried corpse with his 'nails' (the nails of the Crucifixion). Elsewhere in Eliot we have 'Christ the tiger' who comes again in the juvescence of the year, that 'cruellest' resurrection month of April. The continuing prevalence of this theme needs to be stressed in view of objections that have been made to the dove/dive-bomber equation by those who have seen it as an isolated instance of metaphorical gimmickry, and ignored its profound metaphysical consistency. (Note too that in the First World War the German war plane *Taube*, the Dove, was much talked of in England.)

Homing plane and homing Dove leave behind a painfully cleansing fire. Dead leaves (cf. the 'burnt roses' of 55) are blown over the asphalt road: they are 'metal leaves' (*LG* 87) and rattle 'like tin' (*LG* 83) because they are bits of shrapnel left behind by anti-aircraft fire – urban leaves, in fact, blown before 'the urban dawn wind' (*LG* 88). The echoes of Shelley's *Ode to the West Wind* (*LG* 83 and 87, and cf. the 'yellow leaves' of *DS* 128) remind us that Shelley is a poet in mind in the coming encounter, perhaps more especially in line 125 (and see *DS* 52–3). Single-word echoes cannot be easily substantiated, but in cases where the surface meaning is problematical and to 'follow' them leads to rich additional correspondences, the commentator can scarcely ignore them. This said, one may note that the apparently incongruous words

'loitering and hurried' (*LG* 85)

compel one to the kind of brooding which inevitably throws up a recall of Keats's *La Belle Dame sans Merci*. Memory of the parallel encounter with a sadly disenchanted knight, 'palely loitering', is significant since it brings with it images that appropriately cancel out those of the *Burnt Norton* garden –

'The sedge has withered from the lake
And no birds sing.'

Against the background of the bombed city and the smoking ruins this constitutes a telling recall. The word 'hurried', meaning rather disturbed and agitated than in haste, brings overtones of disorder at the planetary, supernatural, and microcosmic levels from forceful usages in Donne (*Good Friday, Riding Westward*, line 5), Shakespeare (*King Lear*, IV, vii, 16) and Milton (*Paradise Lost* V, 775). The contrast with the use of 'unhurried' for the 'Ground swell' of *DS* 36–7 is powerful. (Interesting and relevant reverberations recall from elsewhere in the Eliot canon 'the loitering heirs of city directors', *Waste Land* III, 180, and the highly charged symbolic cry of the Landlord, 'HURRY UP PLEASE ITS TIME', *Waste Land* II.)

While on the subject of single-word echoes one may note that the words 'brown baked', used of the ghost's features (*LG* 94) probably have an even broader allusiveness than the direct association with Dante to which we must soon turn. It is difficult to disentangle the word 'brown' from its established connection in this poem with the edge of the garden pool –

'Dry the pool, dry concrete, brown edged' (*BN* 34)

and with the river of *The Dry Salvages*

'I think that the river
Is a strong brown god . . .' (*DS* 2)

and

'the brown god is almost forgotten' (*DS* 6).

This connection of the colour brown with the edge or frontier of the natural would seem to give it an appropriateness here where we are once more on the edge of the natural. That brown intervenes between red and grey (*EC* 56) suggests perhaps the existence of a thought-out colour symbolism in the *Quartets*. But there are other reasons for regarding 'brown' as an apt word for the features of the returning spectral figure, if single-word echoes are listened to. We may recall Coleridge's ancient mariner,

'For thou art long and lank and brown'

whose delaying hand keeps the wedding-guest shut out from the music and dancing. Perhaps more important, in

view of other, definite Tennysonian echoes, is the hint of
Enoch Arden –

> 'long-bearded, solitary
> Brown, looking hardly human. . .',
> Enoch was so brown, so bow'd' –

returning from his sunbaked exposure to stare at the

> 'square of comfortable light' (cf. *Burnt Norton*),

the window of the happy, might-have-been-recovered home
from which he is now excluded. The description of Annie's
garden, visited at night like Maud's, cannot be ignored in
this connection –

> 'behind
> With one small gate that open'd to the waste
> Flourish'd a little garden square and wall'd
> And in it throve an ancient evergreen,
> A Yew tree . . .'

because later in *Enoch Arden* the emphatic line-opening –

> 'Work without hope'

which *EC* 123, 'wait without hope' may be said to echo,
occurs in connection with Enoch's rigorously sustained self-
discipline of sacrificial withdrawal, so much in key with
Eliot's thinking. The association of Enoch Arden with the
generalized theme of the Wanderer's Return is firm for all
Joyceans (see *Ulysses*, episode 16). The theme of rivalry and
'exclusion' common to *Maud*, *Enoch Arden*, and even the
parable of the Prodigal Son, provides an additional thread in
the associative network. (For further light on 'baked'
see p. 151.)

There is reason to suspect that into this passage Eliot has
intentionally packed a more varied and concentrated accumulation of literary echoes than at any other point in his
work. Grover Smith (in *T. S. Eliot's Poetry and Plays*) has
here identified echoes from Shakespeare, Kipling, Tourneur,
Mallarmé, Milton, Swift, Ford, and Dr Johnson. Not every

reader would accept them all, for the character of the echoing is in tune with the situation and the confrontation: it is haunting but elusive. The problem of firmly identifying the echoes is in line with the problem of identifying the ghost.

One aspect of the elusiveness is, as we have indicated, that Eliot has contrived to give to single words the resonance of a recall or a series of recalls. The strict musical parallel would surely be the 'harmonics' which to the sensitive ear accompany the striking of a single note. Of course no one could prove that such verbal harmonics as these are consciously intended. No one can insist that 'loitering' (*LG* 86) is meant to echo Keats, 'familiar' (*LG* 95) Shakespeare, or 'valediction' (*LG* 148) Donne. We can only insist that the cumulative effect of encountering a sequence of words which seem to ring with harmonics from a richly packed literary past, to which numerous half-identifiable poetic voices contribute, is the perfect stylistic equivalent to the personal confrontation.

For the ghost encountered here is a compound of dead masters. That Dante is especially in Eliot's mind is obvious. In any case Eliot has said so in his talk, *What Dante means to me*, given at the Italian Institute, London, on 4 July 1950, and published in the posthumous volume, *To Criticize the Critic* (Faber and Faber, London 1965).

> 'Twenty years after writing *The Waste Land*, I wrote, in *Little Gidding*, a passage which is intended to be the nearest equivalent to a canto of the Inferno or the Purgatorio, in style as well as content, that I could achieve. The intention, of course, was the same as with my allusions to Dante in *The Waste Land*: to present to the mind of the reader a parallel, by means of contrast, between the Inferno and the Purgatorio, which Dante visited and a hallucinated scene after an air-raid.'

Eliot has a good deal to say in this essay about the difficulty of imitating Dante in English. He also pays tribute to Shelley as an English poet whose mind, saturated in Dante's poetry, 'is inspired to some of the greatest and most

Dantesque lines in English'. He quotes with enthusiasm the passage from Shelley's *Triumph of Life* which describes the meeting with Rousseau and which 'made an indelible impression upon me over forty-five years ago'. (The whole essay is of course worth careful attention for the light it throws on the passage here under consideration.)

Attention should also be drawn to a paper read by C. S. Lewis at Bedford College, London, and published under the title *Shelley, Dryden, and Mr Eliot* in the collection *Rehabilitations and Other Essays* (O.U.P. 1939). In this essay Lewis takes Eliot to task for his alleged underestimate of Shelley and overestimate of Dryden. Lewis draws special attention to the *Triumph of Life* – 'If any passage in our poetry has profited by Dante, it is the unforgettable appearance of Rousseau in that poem. . . .' (p. 28) – and argues that a Milton-plus-Shelley compound would be required to produce an English equivalent to Dante.

The association with Dante in this section relates particularly to Dante's meeting with Brunetto Latini (*Inferno* XV), a meeting firmly recalled by the phrases 'baked features' (*LG* 94) and 'What! are *you* here?' (*LG* 98). Brunetto Latini, a distinguished scholar, was Dante's own teacher, to whom he felt deeply and gratefully indebted for a powerful influence upon him in his early years. Dante finds him among the damned in the Seventh Circle where blasphemers, usurers, and sexual perverts suffer, the perverts afflicted by intermittent rain of Sodomitic fire. In paying tribute to those scholarly mentors and poetic masters from whose teaching and work he had benefited, Eliot faced the same problem as that faced by Dante in paying tribute to Brunetto Latini, the sinner, and Virgil, the pagan. As a committed Christian Eliot recognized his profound indebtedness to teachers and writers who were firmly outside the religious tradition in which he eventually lived and thought and wrote. This is one aspect of the situation here which must necessarily give the confrontation a moral and theological vagueness reflected in the blurring of identity and locale. Paradoxically one may claim that Eliot caters for this vagueness with a subtlety which has its own unique precision.

Another aspect of the situation is that the poet comes to the confrontation in penitential mood, and the penitence does not belong to the moral sphere alone: it has its literary implications. Eliot retracted in middle age the depreciation of Milton to which he committed himself as a young critic, and indeed he seems anxious in *Four Quartets* to reflect his indebtedness to the poets of the nineteenth century whose work had been put out of fashion by the poetic revolution he himself initiated.

We now see something of the moral and psychological complexity for which this confrontation has to cater. The poet's relations with his dead masters, to all of whom he is deeply indebted, must reckon with innumerable distinctions and incongruities. He has always justly revered Virgil and Dante, Shakespeare and Donne. He has perhaps not always been equally just to others. Moreover, there are blasphemers and unbelievers and no doubt perverts among the teachers he has learned from and the artists he was influenced by in his early years. They have all helped to 'save' him, culturally and religiously, even though not all could be logically pictured among the technically 'saved' – or justly given words to speak which their known intellects and personalities would have spurned. All this is brilliantly reckoned with in the blurred instability of approach and response, and in the subtly shifting idiom in which the poet and the compound ghost speak.

As the blurring of identity and relationship in this confrontation serves several purposes, so the collectivity of the compound ghost has implications on other levels than that of purely literary and poetic discipleship. We have established that Dante and Shelley are gathered into this collectivity, and that Brunetto Latini, as the archetypal unsaved mentor, is present too. We must allow that Virgil, Milton, and Shakespeare are allusively involved, and the text will invite us yet to add others to the list. The collectivity thus personified is in accord with Eliot's respect for the collective tradition in cultural and religious life as well as in literary practice. As the poet meets the phantasmal figure, he catches sight of the sudden look 'of some dead master

> 'Whom I had known, forgotten, half recalled
> Both one and many' (*LG* 92–4)

and the reader finds in this image the exact objective correlative for that experience which Eliot's own poetic style recurrently gives him, of catching a sudden clear echo from the style of some 'dead master' of the craft, whose work he has read in the past, known well, forgotten, and can now only half recall. The compound human figure whose appearance, experience, and utterance carry numerous clear characteristics of known but perhaps forgotten personae, is a study in universality which aptly expresses Eliot's basic philosophy of culture, with its emphasis upon the impersonality of the packed authoritative tradition which nourishes the humble, however gifted, and which they in turn may enrich. Eliot's trust in the ordered state, the Catholic faith, and the central orthodoxy of letters, is reliance upon just such a history-packed, authoritative human wisdom (given under divine Providence of course) as is here personified. For full understanding of the richly suggestive episode, one must reckon with the spiritual and the moral, as well as with the intellectual, implications.

In this connection one should note that, in this poem generally, when specifically literary advice is given (in respect of Eliot's poetic craftsmanship), its wording always carries overtones relative to other spheres of public and private life – the political and the social, the religious and the personal. Correspondingly exhortation on the religious level carries verbal overtones which widen the implications towards the sphere of literary practice. There is a two-way traffic over the social, literary, and religious areas. This is what gives Eliot's poetry on the one hand its impressive unity and power, on the other hand its exciting variety of

dimension and subtlety of texture. And indeed, just as
Eliot's poetic utterance continually makes relationships
between the social, religious, and literary areas of experience, so too it makes relationships between the various
aspects of human action and response within each of these
fields. In other words, it is not just that Eliot relates the
literary tradition to the religious tradition, the authority of
the one to the authority of the other, the personal demand
of the one to the personal demand of the other; he also
relates the various aspects of literary life, objective and subjective, collective and individual, public and vocational, in
a unified pattern of purpose and demand, social meaning and
personal vocation, in which everything has its place. Hence
he finds it desirable to write about the purpose of education
as well as, say, about the best way of mastering one's craft in
the choice of words for poetic composition. One may add
that this inner unity in multiplicity is equally evident from
the religious as from the literary angle. *Four Quartets* bring
together the dogmatic and the mystical, the institutional and
the personal, the sacramental and the disciplinary, in a
pattern of Christian exploration which affirms life powerfully and positively from the Christian position. At the heart
of the reconciliation, philosophically and historically, dog-
matically and personally, is the Word made flesh. Here
again, in this compound ghost of historic poethood, the
word is made flesh. It is logical, therefore, that even this
essentially poetic phantom should carry with him faintly-
sensed associations of the risen Christ, half-recognized in
the dimness before dawn. And it is equally logical that the
figure should speak authoritatively, not only with the voice
of a poet experienced in his craft and of a fellow-being who
has lived and suffered and learned but also with the accents
of a spiritual director.

The semi-paradoxical adjectives, 'familiar', 'compound',
'intimate', and 'unidentifiable' (*LG* 95–6) and the corresponding phrases, 'he a face still forming' (*LG* 101) and
'Too strange to each other for misunderstanding' (*LG* 104),

used against the background of 'meeting nowhere, no before and after' (*LG* 106), together accurately constitute the required personification of authoritative tradition and the flavour of the humble individual's encounter with it. The individual's capacity to detach himself from his own personality and achievement in the face of this encounter with the universal which has nourished each and all, is represented in the poet's awareness of the 'double part' (*LG* 97) he plays and the multiplicity of his voices. For just as the construction of the universal master out of the numerous characters whom he represents and who may represent him is the work of the *moment*, the point of intersection, and is hard to achieve and sustain, so the construction of the true individual human personality out of the innumerable particularities of temporal successiveness requires an act of the will.

While the predominant significance of the dead master is as a representative of the collective cultural tradition and of the poetic tradition especially, one may note in parenthesis that the concept of a 'compound' being, involving a multiplicity of persons, inevitably carries overtones of the Trinity. These overtones are evident in lines 92–5, where the words 'master' and 'ghost' (Holy Ghost) are heard and where there is a suggestion of bread (the Bread of Life) in the words 'brown baked'. (The prodigal son, wearying of feeding on the husks of swine, returned home in search of the true bread available in abundance even to his father's servants. Cf. *LG* 116.)

In asking the question 'What! are *you* here?' (*LG* 98), with its compressed reaction of wonder, recognition, and uncertain interrogation, the poet establishes communication. His words do not result from recognition of the master: rather they precede and 'compel' recognition (*LG* 102). Thus communication between the individual and the traditional wisdom is based on the individual's commitment in humility, familiarity (acquaintanceship), and inquiry (search, knowledge). It is the 'common wind' (*LG* 103) of ordinary, unromantic (indeed, *pedestrian!*) experience which blows them together. The implication here is that within the ordinariness of the temporal course, contact with any great representative of the past, in reading especially, may constitute a fruitful supra-temporal point of intersection. Meeting representatives of the past thus, we escape the misunderstandings which fog our relationships with our contemporaries, and which are due to our shared inability fully to escape the prejudices of our own age, which, whether we succumb to them or react against them, queer the pitch of contemporaneous relationships. It is thus easier to establish 'concord' (*LG* 105) by the very transcendence of finite contemporaneousness, in a supra-temporal, supra-local 'intersection time/Of meeting nowhere, no before and after' (*LG* 105–6). Though the two tread the same pavement (*LG* 107), it is not in a living patrol.

The blending of awe with familiarity is the note of the poet's initial response. He is full of 'wonder' (*LG* 108), yet not uncomfortable; on the contrary, at ease; and this ease is itself surprising. Encounter with the personified tradition, though it naturally stirs one to awe, also arouses the sense of being at home. Humbly the poet admits his limitations, 'I may not comprehend' (*LG* 110), using a word highly charged for Eliot by his frequent hearing of the Last Gospel ('And the Light shineth in darkness; and the darkness comprehended it not', St John I, 5), which, as a focal summary of the Incarnation leaves its mark ubiquitously in the poem in the use of the word 'Word' and is also specifically echoed in *BN* 116 and 135.

The dead master has little to say to Eliot (the poet) about their common craft. He does not choose to talk about his 'thought and theory': they have 'served their purpose' (*LG* 113). So have Eliot's own. The proper attitude to one's past poetic achievement is to ask forgiveness of others for 'both bad and good' (*LG* 116). Thus the ethos of a developed Christian morality and spirituality is made applicable to the sphere of poetic practice. One does not evaluate one's past work in an attitude of mingled self-congratulation and self-blame: one regards the whole in a penitential spirit, since one has fed on a freely given tradition and trust in order to produce the good (which good is itself, after all, only a 'recovery') and has abused the tradition and trust in producing the bad. Over the centuries, then, as between poet and poet, there must be mutual forgiveness asked and given. Humbly the poet must accept his temporal placing: as last year's problems of poetic expression are tied to last year's problems of what had then to be said, so next year's problems of poetic expression will be tied to next year's problems of what will then have to be said. Neither of these issues now concerns the poet whose work is done. There is humour, perhaps, as well as grave morality, in the image of the 'full-fed beast' kicking the bucket, *LG* 117. The fact that this image follows immediately on the exhortation to interchange forgiveness surely strengthens the continuing thread of allusions to the parable of the Prodigal Son. Forgiveness is to be interchanged and the fatted calf is to be killed. But the spirit of the dead master, still 'unappeased' (*LG* 121: and cf. 'Appeasing', *BN* 51) – still, that is, in a purgatorial state – and wandering freely between two closely resembling worlds, returns to streets he never expected to revisit when he died 'on a distant shore'. The ambiguities here are to be noted, for Eliot's surface vagueness always calls for multiple readings. The 'two worlds become much like each other' (*LG* 122) may well mean the world of the dead master's own lifetime and the twentieth century, but probably much more surely means the purgatorial condition and the condition of twentieth-century life generally and of wartime London in particular.

Although we have already said that the body left on a 'distant shore' (*LG* 125) may well be Shelley's, this identification would not exclude other references, contemporary or literary. Readers of *In Memoriam* might feel that Tennyson's Hallam, if not Tennyson himself, is now a distinct presence too. A further connection that must be mentioned is that between the meeting here and Aeneas's encounter with the ghost of Palinurus in the underworld in *Aeneid* VI. Palinurus, the pilot, was lost overboard in a heavy storm and his body was left unburied on a distant shore. He too is now an 'unappeased' spirit wandering among the restless crowd who cannot be transported across the river Cocytus until their bones lie quiet in the earth (*Aeneid* VI, 325 ff.). The connection is important (like so many of Eliot's allusions in this poem) not so much in itself as because of the cumulative effect of a series of scattered allusions to which it must be related. For the crowd of restless, unburied ghosts inhabiting the transitional underworld (world not world) are described by Virgil in wintry images of falling leaves and gathering birds –

> quam multa in silvis autumni frigore primo
> lapsa cadunt folia, aut ad terram gurgite ab alto
> quam multae glomerantur aves, ubi frigidus annus
> trans pontum fugat –

(*Aeneid* VI, 309–12)

which have already been faintly recalled in the

'Men and bits of paper, whirled by the cold wind' (*BN* 104)

and the 'twittering world' (*BN* 113) of London's underground underworld, also a 'world not world' (*BN* 116), and therefore a world 'between two worlds' (*LG* 122). The oblique connection between the blown leaves (flak) of this wartime patrol (*LG* 87) and the blown men and bits of paper of London's more normal life further strengthens a network of related allusions and cross-references whose total effect is perhaps chiefly to add to our sense of the sad unreality of civilization as pictured in *BN* III.

It should be added that each such network of allusions, whether to Virgil, Dante, and Shakespeare, or to lesser poets like Shelley, Tennyson, and Longfellow, feeds into our experience of reading the sense of involvement in a pilgrimage of epic dimensions whose universality makes it relevant in all ages to all conditions of men. But we must be careful to note the different functions which rich allusiveness may perform, in particular, here, the difference between combining together many poets in the composite study of past poethood, which is a dominating aspect of the ghost's multi-personal role, and involving the experience of litera-ture alongside the experience of life in Eliot's own record of a pilgrimage. Eliot's situation here, as the poet, is being paralleled with Aeneas's, not with Virgil's. The correspon-dences with Dante are complicated because Dante is the central figure of *The Divine Comedy* as well as the maker of a body of poetry. This complexity attaches to echoes of Tennyson's *In Memoriam* too. In the case of lyric poets like Donne, the assumed identity of poet as maker and poet as speaker (in *The Ecstasy* for instance) may serve for working purposes; but the assumption is a rough one and should be open to scrutiny. This, no doubt, is one of the issues in the background to the strange lines –

'So I assumed a double part, and cried
And heard another's voice cry: "What! are *you* here?"
Although we were not.' (*LG* 97–9)

to which we must return for further consideration later. (See p. 175.) Meantime it is worth saying that in his recorded reading Eliot himself firmly emphasizes the 'I' of line 97.

The dead master's message is heavy with irony. He and Eliot have shared the common concern with speech; they therefore strove to purify the language of their peoples; they were also driven to prophetic exhortation in the effort to open the eyes of their generations to the significance of their history and their destiny, of their origin and their end ('urge the mind to aftersight and foresight'). The master therefore now discloses the rewards which old age will bring to the poet-prophet who has spent his life in this effort to cleanse his age's utterance and open its eyes to the truth. These rewards, the three 'gifts reserved for age', are the last stages of physical, intellectual, and spiritual development. Physic-ally the ageing poet must face in disillusionment the 'cold friction' of the failing senses, as appetites are still teased, but without the prospect of satisfaction. This friction, all that is left of the 'trilling wire' which sang in the blood (*BN* 49), leads only to the 'bitter tastelessness of shadow fruit' (*LG* 133): and the mockery of nourishment at the end of fallen man's life in the flesh takes us back mentally to Eve's bite in the 'bitter apple' (*DS* 117) which is at the root of human self-centredness, and of the inevitable painful severence at the gradual falling asunder of body and soul (*LG* 134). Mentally the ageing poet must be teased by powerless anger, by tormenting humourless laughter, as he becomes increasingly aware of human folly and its absurdity (and cf. *LG* 66–9). Thirdly, the poet must suffer the remorse of reliving his past experience. He will know the shame of recognizing too late his own past motives for what they really were, and seeing that certain actions were evil and intentionally damaging to others, though at the time he had deceived himself into the belief that they were virtuous. In this last condition, the approval of fools, that is presumably the noisy appreciation of his work by men who fail to understand it, will sting, and the conferment of honours for his misunderstood and wrongly-assessed achievement will but add to his guilt.

The human spirit, exasperated thus by the closure of satisfying physical life, by disillusionment with the world, with others, and with itself, will proceed 'from wrong to wrong', tormented alternately by its own evil and by the evil of others, unless it is 'restored' by the cleansing fire. The 'refining fire' (*LG* 145) is the fire of divine love and mercy in its disciplinary manifestations, whether as the burning pyre of sacrifice on which the selfish self is immolated (cf. *LG* 205), or as the purgatorial flames which the unappeased spirit encounters hereafter. Restoration involves learning to subordinate one's own thoughts and acts to that pattern of divine purpose in which each humble individual plays his part like a dancer in the cosmic dance.

The word 'figured', with its overtones of dancing, much

enriched for those acquainted with *The Governour*, has been used already so as to give it associations with the ordered, harmonious patterning of the universe (*BN* 54) and with that which is clearly outlined by the light (*BN* 57). The use here therefore of the word 'disfigured' (*LG* 147) is evocative of contrasting disorder and darkness. The ghost's departure is described to echoes of Shakespeare (for Octavius kept his sword at Philippi 'like a dancer', *Antony and Cleopatra* III, xi, 36), and old Hamlet's Ghost 'faded on the crowing of the cock' (*Hamlet* I, i, 157). The 'horn' is presumably the All-Clear of the air-raid siren; though the first morning movement of motor traffic is no doubt in mind too.

That the compound ghost should be thus plainly assoc-iated with the spirit whom Hamlet encounters on the battlements adds to his status as a peregrine visitant from another world who brings perhaps 'airs from heaven', per-haps 'blasts from hell', but more likely winds from both and from purgatory too; for this reading would give point to the fact that the poet is walking 'between three districts whence the smoke arose' (*LG* 85). If we do not know already, we shall know by the end of *LG* IV that there are fires and fires, appropriate to hell and to purgatory, and by the end of *LG* V that there are fires appropriate to heaven too. Uncertainty about the ghost's character and source is fitting. It is true that he makes no great claims for himself; but he speaks like one having authority, he speaks from wisdom and know-ledge which seem to be not only composite but universal, and he cannot therefore be diminished by reference to the limitations of any of the individual personae whose voices we detect in him.

The link with *Hamlet* here is one which we should carry forward in our minds to the further consideration of echoes from *Hamlet* in the next movement (*LG* 170–1. See p. 166). At the same time it would be relevant to carry forward, too, the hint of Donne's memorable title *A Valediction, Forbid-ding Mourning*, which some readers will pick up from among the overtones of *LG* 148. The association with *Antony and*

Cleopatra must also be regarded as more than an isolated enrichment of the poem's texture in view of what is to follow in *LG* IV (see p. 169).

Meantime it will clarify our thinking at the end of this remarkable episode if we bear in mind the danger of over-simplifying the parallels that allusions seem to have established. The poet, meeting the ghost, has been compared to Dante (in his own poem) meeting Brunetto Latini and to Aeneas (in Virgil's poem) meeting Palinurus. The ghost himself, because he is a composite study in the masters to whom Eliot is indebted, sums up in himself the writers from whom Eliot has learned – including Dante and Virgil and many who are nameless. (Notice how Dante is doubly involved here.) It is not therefore strictly accurate to say that the ghost represents Brunetto Latini. Rather he represents the masters who have influenced Eliot in the way that Brunetto Latini influenced Dante. On the other hand we may well admit that the ghost represents Virgil both in the sense that Eliot learned from Virgil the poet and in the sense that Virgil is a character in *The Divine Comedy* who gives guidance to the archetypally searching and penitent poet.

III

There are three conditions which often look alike

After the austere judgements and stern disciplinary demands contained in the later lines of Movement II, the poet once more finds it desirable to forestall possible misunderstanding by any who might be tempted to read a purely negative, ascetic, or Stoical posture into his utterance. Above all, therefore, he must make clear that the demand for self-surrender, self-transcendence, and rejection of what is traditionally called 'worldliness' is something different from escapism, indifference, or apathy. He admits that it is not easy to distinguish between the three conditions here at issue; for they 'flourish in the same hedgerow' (*LG* 151).

The three are attachment, detachment, and indifference. In 1937, in his Preface to Djuna Barnes's *Nightwood*, Eliot wrote –

> 'It seems to me that all of us, so far as we attach ourselves to created objects and surrender our wills to temporal ends, are eaten by the same worm.'

In seeking to achieve the true detachment which will save us from the worm, we must avoid the peril of merely falling into indifference. There is a vitality about attachment, the vitality of the stinging weed, the nettle. Death kills the weed and takes away the sting. Between live and dead nettle flourishes the 'unflowering' indifference. What turns attachment into indifference is a negative contraction of concern – the turning away of human interest from 'self' and from 'things' and from 'persons' (*LG* 153). What turns attachment into true detachment is a positive *expansion* of concern – the 'liberation' of human interest from limited attention to 'self' and to 'things' and to 'persons'. Memory, properly used (for there is a time for the 'evening with the photograph album', *EC* 199), will not be a means of pinning our affections to the past. Regret, which fastens the mind on the past, and desire, which fastens the mind on the future (also a 'faded song', *DS* 126), are both servitudes. Memory, used as here in this poem, can liberate us from both servitudes. The essential thing is that attachment has to be expanded into love, not obliterated by indifference. The illustration given is that of love of a country growing out of 'attachment to our own field of action' but becoming something so free of self-interest that the attachment gradually loses its importance – not by being denied, but by being transcended. Thus the concern with history, whether private or public, whether one's personal past or the nation's cultural and political past, may be a tyranny or a liberation, according to whether we allow the concern with the past to fix our attachments or to expand them into love. This process of expanding attachment into love corresponds to the process of expanding desire into love: for attachment is past-orientated as desire is future-orientated. All interests, personal and public, must be transcended, not by obliteration, but by *transfiguration*. The faces and places we loved, as far as our selfishness allowed us to love, 'vanish' (*LG* 163) as the objects of personal attachment because they have been handed over to take their part, like the disciplined self, in the great cosmic dance which is the pattern of the divine purpose, and which renews all that is involved in it. Once more the key word *figure* is notable. The bombing 'disfigured' the street (*LG* 147). This was not the way to turn our attachment to the street into something greater. This was the way of indifference. The places, like the faces, must be 'transfigured' (*LG* 165).

Eliot endeavours in this passage to set the record straight. It should be impossible for any critic who has studied it to repeat the foolish charge that Eliot was a reactionary following 'an antique drum'.

Sin is Behovely

The natural question now facing poet and reader is whether Eliot's optimism is too optimistic: that is to say, whether the image of the dance in which all creation is joined in worship, as being the final end, does not offend by leaving open the question – Can evil and suffering be thus neatly brushed under the philosophical carpet? Everyone who has ever seriously pondered the Christian Faith has had to reckon with this problem. Dame Julian of Norwich, the fourteenth-century mystic, faced it in her *Revelations of Divine Love*. How could one reconcile the goodness of God with the presence of sin in the world? Jesus spoke to her in a vision, saying: 'Synne is behovabil, but al shal be wel & al shal be wel & al manner of thyng shal be wel.' Eliot repeats her words, by 'All shall be well' (*LG* 167) no doubt meaning not only that everything shall be satisfactory, but also that all the sick patients from the earthly hospital of *East Coker* IV shall be restored to health. (And the late realization of this continuing theme throws back an additional connotative dimension on the use of the words 'recover' and 'recovery' in such lines as *EC* 186. 'There is only the fight to recover . . .' health, presumably, as well as 'what has been lost'.)

It is interesting that Eliot should choose to use here (*LG* 165 ff.) a revelatory message rather than to argue the issue out in logical thoroughness. It might be protested that in this case he too readily relies on a familiarity among the cultured with the doctrine at issue. From the days of St Augustine it has been argued that, since the Fall of Man led to the Redemption of Man in Christ, and since the latter was a divine act of love to which men must respond with overflowing gratitude and joy, there is a sense in which, after the event, man may paradoxically look back in thankfulness to the sin of Eve whose 'consequences' were an act so wonderful. (*O felix culpa!*) This argument states, we may say, in mythical terms, the Christian conviction that the experience of divine forgiveness after penitence is so much a cause of joy and gratitude that, after the event, the forgiven penitent may look back with a degree of paradoxically logical thankfulness on the sin whose 'consequences' have eventually proved so joyful. In this sense even sin may be said to have a place in the whole pattern when that pattern is fully realizable. Sin therefore is 'behovely', that is, not without its due part in the total pattern in which, ultimately, 'all manner of thing shall be well' (*LG* 168).

The importance here of proving the Fall of Man to be after all a *felix culpa* is that by implication this proof sheds a new light on corresponding events – the English Civil strife which cast out emigrants to America, as well as the poet's own sins in the past. These too can be seen as 'behovely' when subsumed into the pattern of the universal dance. This is the philosophical mode of reconciliation which balances the historical mode of reconciliation. It is therefore an appropriate basis for the poet's further reflections, here at Little Gidding, on the people who were divided by strife in the Civil War of the seventeenth century and who are now united, in our eyes, by their involvement in the same struggle at the same point of history. Eliot's thoughts turn from Charles I, the 'king' who came here 'at nightfall' (*LG* 175) to 'three men, and more, on the scaffold'. Attempts to identify the 'three men' (e.g. as Strafford, Laud, and Charles himself on the one side, and as executed or persecuted leaders on the other side) are perhaps reasonable, but the word 'three' is immediately weakened by the phrase 'and more', so that one may well ask why the apparently loose wording is used. The answer is that Eliot wishes to make the correspondence with the three crosses of the Crucifixion. It should be added that the use of the word 'nightfall' here, as of 'smokefall' – *BN* 87, considered in relation to other numerous uses of the word 'fall' in the poem, leaves one persuaded that Eliot is thus faintly echoing the word 'Fall'. He is once more pressing the parallel between the Fall which shut Adam out of Paradise after the Luciferian Fall and the War in Heaven, and the Civil War from which emigrants went out of England. The faint, but unignorable, presence of Milton in this Quartet inevitably carries with it overtones of *Paradise Lost*, so that thoughts of the Fall and of the need to 'justify the ways of God to men' cannot be evaded.

Whether or not Grover Smith is right in saying that Eliot alludes both to Milton and to Joyce in his reference to one 'who died blind and quiet' (*LG* 179), it would surely be a mistake to limit references here to men who were involved in the seventeenth-century conflict. Rather Eliot seems already to have broadened his range of reference by the calculated vagueness we have noted in *LG* 176–8. Indeed, repeated re-readings of the poem as a whole make it as difficult *not* to picture the crucified King of the Jews in the darkness (the 'king at nightfall', *LG* 175) as not to picture the three crosses in the succeeding line. For we have already, on one or two occasions in reading the *Quartets*, stood momentarily, through the effects of a sudden verbal stab, at the foot of the Cross as darkness falls. The carrying away of the Sun/Son by a black cloud (*BN* 128) represents an inescapable equation simply on the basis of Light and Cloud imagery throughout the poem. The setting of the Sun/Son and the rising of the Sun/Son represents a firm pun for readers of Donne's *Good Friday, Riding Westwards*, so often alluded to in this poem. (See *DS* 175–6.) Moreover, one must voice the irrepressible, if subjective, view that it is impossible for a sensitive writer to spend as much time in the literary company of Donne and Joyce as Eliot did without this kind of ambiguity becoming second nature to him.

The aptness of these allusions (*LG* 175–6) is that they bring together, under the shelter of the beheaded king's martyrdom and the crucified King's martyrdom, the friend and the foe, the forgiven and saved sinner and the impenitent unbelieving one (the two thieves at Christ's sides). The importance of such an emphasis on a reconciliation which not only involves saved royalist and saved rebel, but also reaches out to involve saved penitent and 'saved' impenitent, or saved believer and saved unbeliever, is that it connects logically with the proclamation that 'Sin is behovely' (*LG* 166), inevitable in the very scheme of things, and casts thus a faint gleam of hope backward for those still troubled over the destiny of Brunetto Latini and his like.

Why, the poet asks, should we 'celebrate/These dead men more than the dying?' and there is a double edge to the word 'dying' which turns the question into a two-dimensional one. Why should we celebrate those dead in this ancient conflict instead of concentrating on those who are now dying in the Second World War? And why should we celebrate the dead more than the dying – that is, more than the living, for the presently alive are the future's dead and therefore, from the supra-temporal angle, the distinction is not between live and dead, but between dying and dead. (The paradox that the living are really the dying has been before us several times and with a variety of emphases. We sum up some of its deeper implications when we reach the more explicit formulation of the theme in the last movement. See *LG* 228 ff. 'We die with the dying' and our commentary on p. 173.) The answer to both questions is the same. It is not a matter of trying to turn the clock back (ring 'backward' the 'bell' of *DS* I) or of raising a fire alarm. ('The alarm called "ringing the bell backward" is sounded by striking a peal of bells up the scale, beginning with the bass', Grover Smith, p. 293.) Nor is it for the purpose of sentimentally reviving the Stuart cause, which would be like trying to exist in the fantastic dream world of the Spectral Rose (cf. the Ballet of that name). The implication is that the universal dance is not an artificially contrived ballet performed against the theatrical 'panorama' and 'façade' which time rolls away (see *EC* 113–17). There is nothing precious or escapist about the interest in history. We cannot revive the ideological struggles of the past, whether political or religious. Though men must be restored, policies belong to their own time. To follow an 'antique drum' (as we did when we stopped to listen to the 'weak pipe and the little drum' in *EC* I, 26) is merely to take ourselves back into a dream world. The rival contenders in the English Civil War, Royalist and Republican who struggled for different constitutions, now accept the same 'constitution', the constitution of silence in which their specific ideologies are no longer propagated. The same party embraces them. 'Party' too is double-edged. One may take the word in a legal sense, as of a person, therefore a Person, a divine Person whose arms are folded around them. This reading is confirmed later by the complex connotation of the word 'infolded' which occurs at the final climax of the poem, *LG* 257, when it is clear that the image of a sheepfold is allusively involved in the beatific vision. In a poem as richly harmonized as *Four Quartets* you cannot have the presence of a sheepfold without that of the Shepherd, or indeed the presence of the Shepherd without the recovery of the lost sheep. Thus 'folded in a single party' (*LG* 191) may justifiably be read in the light of the final in-folding – and we are further strengthened in our reading of Crucifixion echoes in *LG* 175–6. And if we read 'folded' as carrying the additional connotation, however faint, of 'gathered into a fold', then it is difficult not to allow 'party' the further additional connotation of a feast. These lighter harmonics must be recognized by any reader who has picked up the overtones of the Prodigal Son and of *Maud* and has threaded into them the theme of exclusion from music and dancing which has been firmly if fitfully with us since the close of *East Coker* I – and indeed since the first echo from Sir John Davies's *Orchestra* if we are familiar with the poem.

Lines 192–5 are so punctuated as to allow a dual syntactical role to line 193. Eliot is saying – Whatever we may have inherited from the conquerors, we have certainly inherited a symbol from the conquered. He is also saying – Whatever we inherit from the conquerors is also an inheritance from the conquered. All have bequeathed us what they all had to leave us; the symbol of enmities reconciled in death, attachments transfigured by death. Thus death too has its positive function in relation to the final end in which 'all shall be well'. Eliot returns to Dame Julian of Norwich, quoting in conclusion from her fourteenth revelation in which our Lord says to her –

> 'I am Ground of thy beseeching; first it is my will that thou have it; and after, I make thee to will it; and since I make thee to beseech it and thou beseechest it, how should it then be that thou shouldst not have thy beseeching?'*

This 'shewing' may be called a justification of Christian trust, more especially trust in God's mercy. God is declared to provide the impulse which drives man to prayer for mercy. It is God's will that man should find mercy. It is therefore God's will that man should want mercy. It is therefore God's will that man should pray for mercy. It is therefore logically inescapable that God should grant mercy. Man's task therefore is not to supply the impulse but to purify his motive, so that the whole circuit or pattern of divine action in this

* *Revelations of Divine Love*, ed. Dom. Roger Huddleston, London, Burns Oates. (Page 72.)

respect may be worked out and not marred by an insertion of ulterior human selfishness into what is, after all, one more instance of the dance – the pattern of love.

Before leaving this movement we must look back at the odd cluster of apparent echoes of *Hamlet* in lines 170–1, where the rapid sequence of the words 'commendable', 'kin', and 'kindness' recalls very memorable lines in Act I, scene ii of the play,

> 'A little more than kin and less than kind',
>
> (line 65)

and

> 'Tis sweet and commendable in your nature, Hamlet,
> To give these mourning duties to your father',
>
> (lines 87–8).

This cluster introduces a complex of relevant associations. At the point in question Hamlet is being criticized for being far too inclined to mourn the dead and indeed to idealize the murdered king (cf. the poet and Charles I), and he is soon to be burdened by the problem of trying to reconcile himself to the inheritance of bloodshed. Hamlet, like the poet, receives a spectral visitation from the other world. Since the compound ghost departed to a firm echo of the departure of Old Hamlet's ghost (*LG* 149) there can be no doubt that the elaborate parallelism is intentional. What makes the correspondence even more subtle is that the compound ghost also departed to a fainter echo of the memorable title, *A Valediction, Forbidding Mourning*. Once more it is not the presence of any one given allusion which enables one to press the associative implications with confidence but rather the gathered cluster of scattered echoes. The gathering in of the cluster which enables the reader to establish (or rather to 'recover') the meaning of the poem is itself parallel to the gathering in of scattered moments which enables man to recover the meaning of existence.

One must here add that re-readings also blend the shadowy recall of King Duncan, effected by faint overtones from *Macbeth* (e.g. *DS* 128, *DS* 39, 41, and 48), into the now clearly articulated theme of the murdered or martyred king. (Remember Mary Queen of Scots too.)

Now that the detection of echoes from *Hamlet* has justified itself, we may properly look back to *DS* 114, the cry *de profundis*, 'People change, and smile', and note the faint recall of Hamlet's disillusionment ('That one may smile, and smile, and be a villain', I, v, 108), important because it suddenly deepens the emotional and philosophical texture immeasurably by ranging the agony of evil alongside the agony of suffering. No doubt those who read into *Hamlet* something of the archetypal significance which the play is given in *Ulysses*, and trace the pattern of Fall and Original Sin in the corruption of Gertrude and the inherited guilt of the Prince, will find that the references further enrich the poem's orchestration. But without necessarily pressing the matter as far as that, one may justifiably add Hamlet to the list of those whose dilemma leaves them only the choice of 'fire or fire' (*LG* 213), as presented in the next movement.

IV

The dove descending breaks the air

This lyric directly introduces the Holy Spirit as the corresponding movements of *Burnt Norton*, *East Coker*, and *The Dry Salvages* brought in God the Creator, Christ the Redeemer, and the Virgin Mary. St John the Baptist saw the Spirit 'descending from heaven like a dove' upon Christ (St John I, 32), and this image, combined with that of the pentecostal tongues of flame, is blended with the destructive descent of the dive-bomber. The bomber's 'discharge' is an explosive incendiary load which will burn out 'sin and error' – giving us the one possible 'discharge' from our debt of guilt. The fire of God's redeeming love which will burn away our worldliness is the only alternative to the fire of selfish desire. The hope/despair paradox is pressed once more. Our only hope is the destruction of worldly hope

('hope for the wrong thing', *EC* 124) – despair of self and of the world, in fact. We burn either in self-love or in sacrificial self-immolation. The use of the word 'pyre' (*LG* 205) may recall Dido's self-immolation in the fire which saved her from the torment of thwarted passion, but its primary reference no doubt is to the pyre of Heracles, whose apotheosis is plainly alluded to in the next stanza.

The echo of *Coriolanus* in lines 206 and 213 ('One fire drives out one fire; one nail, one nail', *Coriolanus* IV, vii, 54) is interesting both because Coriolanus's dilemma powerfully recapitulates the painful either/or implicit in the human situation as presented here, and because the fire image is linked by it to the nail image, which elsewhere in Eliot (*Waste Land* 75) marks an allusion to the Crucifixion (see p. 142).

Who then devised the torment? Love

It is in accord with Eliot's poetic practice that he should follow a stanza in which divine love is seen operating among men like a dive-bomber over wartime London, with a stanza in which divine love is seen operating like a magical blood-drenched shirt of classical legend. In the course of the story, the centaur Nessus, having safely carried Heracles's wife Deianira across a river, then tried to rape her. Heracles shot him with a poisoned arrow. In death Nessus gave some of his blood to Deianira, telling her that it had strange power to arouse love. Long afterwards, when Heracles proved unfaithful to Deianira, she gave him a shirt soaked in this blood. As soon as Heracles put it on, it began to burn him, and to escape the intolerable pain Heracles climbed on a funeral pyre on Mount Oeta and destroyed himself by fire. Thus as Deianira, out of her love for Heracles, made the 'shirt of flame' which tormented him till he chose self-sacrifice on the pyre, and thereby achieved apotheosis, so the divine Love lies behind the suffering inherent in the human situation, the suffering which compels us to choose between self-love and self-sacrifice. The 'intolerable' burden of selfishness is a burning garment which we cannot ourselves remove: so too is the 'intolerable' burden of altruistic passion, or the burden of a Hamlet, who recognizes his close dependence on usurping evil. The poet's burden in trying to assimilate 'the torment of others' (*DS* 112) or reconcile himself to past suffering and conflict (*LG* III) is another such divinely devised torment. We cannot ourselves tear off the burning garment. 'Human power' (*LG* 211) is unequal to the task. Only divine Grace will do.

At this point we may appropriately recall the echo of *Antony and Cleopatra* (*LG* 146) heard at the moment of the compound ghost's leave-taking (see p. 157). The Antony who claimed that at the Battle of Philippi his present enemy Caesar 'kept his sword e'en like a dancer' soon after finds himself trapped between his passion for an apparently treacherous Cleopatra and his defeat by Caesar. 'The shirt of Nessus is upon me,' he cries (IV, xiii, 43), comparing his dilemma with that of his supposed ancestor, Heracles. And it is not long before he is also comparing Cleopatra's destiny and his with that of 'Dido and her Aeneas' (IV, xiv, 53). As Eliot has already plainly quoted *Antony and Cleopatra* (*LG* 146) the recall here of his exclamation about the shirt of Nessus and of the personal dilemma which produced the cry, is a natural one. Antony is thus added to Coriolanus and Hamlet in that very mixed company of shadowy participants in the choice of fire or fire.

Thus this powerful lyric, read in the light of past pre-echoes, ties together a number of thematic threads by virtue of its far-reaching allusiveness. The classical-mythological sequence which has been fitfully with us, more especially perhaps in Virgilian echoes, seems to reach a point of finality in the apotheosis of Heracles and the immolation of Dido, the two consuming and consumed human passions like burnt roses leaving their smoke in the air. Over against this, the more affirmative voice of Julian of Norwich is detected again in a clear echo ('Who then devised the torment? Love.' *LG* 207) of the last chapter of her *Revelations*, where she records how God finally made the purpose of all his 'shewings' known to her.

'I was answered in ghostly understanding, saying thus: "Wouldst thou witten (know) thy Lord's meaning in this thing? Wit it well: Love was his meaning. Who shewed it thee? Love. Wherefore shewed it he? For Love"', p. 169.

Moreover, as the presence of the Holy Spirit in this lyric balances the presence of Christ in *East Coker* IV and that of the Virgin Mary in *Dry Salvages* IV, so too the emphasis on the descent of the Dove (and it is worth recalling that Eliot's friend Charles Williams wrote his history of the Holy Spirit in the Church under the title, *The Descent of the Dove*), on the pentecostal tongues of flame, and on the power given to the apostles to grant 'discharge from sin' (*LG* 203), inevitably alludes to the Apostolic Succession, the Episcopacy in whose defence King Charles is claimed to have been martyred, and to the authority of absolution vested in the priesthood.

'And when he had said this, he breathed on them, and saith unto them, Receive ye the Holy Ghost: Whose soever sins ye remit, they are remitted unto them; and whose soever sins ye retain, they are retained.' (St John XX, 22–3)

Knowing what Eliot's religious practices were, one must not ignore – though of course one must not exaggerate – the allusive references here to the continuing institutional life of the Church in ordination and absolution; for the words of the one discharge (given above) are recited by the bishop as he ordains a priest.

We now see that the four lyrics which stand as the fourth movements of the *Quartets* have touched allusively on moments in the institutional life of the Church at which the eternal intersects the temporal – in the utterance of the Word and the burial of the dead (*BN* IV), in the sacrament of the Mass (*EC* IV), in the self-offering of prayer and more particularly at the ringing of the Angelus (*DS* IV), and in the granting of absolution and the ordaining of priests (*LG* IV).

These acts give order, pattern, and meaning, and involve the operation of the Word. In the same way, poetry itself gives order, pattern, and meaning to experience through the operation of the Word. Ideally poetry may be said to be related to other human utterance as the Church's practices should be related to other forms of action. (This is not a comprehensive definition of anything, but an aspect of the total system of patterns explored by the poet.) It is appropriate, therefore, to match the concentrated and conscious acts of the Church with a concentrated and conscious 'poetry' – a poetic poetry, if you like, which has a high degree of organization and a high level of cultivated symbolism. Thus the style and character of the four fourth movements matches their meaning and function. The formality and intensity of these lyrics is itself a miracle of fitness.

It remains to add that, in terms of the long spiritual pilgrimage from the *Burnt Norton* garden, the note of absolution, distinctly sounded here, is as crucial (if not as explicit) as the call to self-surrender heard in *Dry Salvages* II or the note of penitence echoed in *Little Gidding* II (*LG* 114–15).

V

What we call the beginning is often the end

Eliot returns appropriately in his last movement to the beginning–end equation. To 'make an end', i.e., to define a goal, is obviously to make a start. Turning over a new leaf is also to make both an end and a beginning. Still carrying in mind the lingering reverberations of the powerful 'discharge' in the last movement (*LG* 203), with its crucial reference to absolution, we may also read that to repent and to receive absolution is to die unto sin and be reborn in Christ and thus to recapitulate the sacrament of Baptism and repeat the pattern of crucifixion, burial, and resurrection. It is to 'put off' the old man and put on the new (and the emphatic line-end of *LG* 42 resonates again in this realization).

Over these more obvious paradoxes hang other associations. As the Old Testament opens with the words, 'In the beginning God . . .' (two sentences before the 'Spirit of God moved upon the face of the waters', cf. *BN* 35), so the Gospel of St John opens with the words, 'In the beginning was the Word . . .' God is Alpha and Omega, the beginning and the ending, first cause and final cause, origin and end of all things. A patterned unity runs through all creation. It is the central principle even of this present undertaking, this poem, determining alike its construction and its vocabulary. (The principle may be illustrated by comparing the shape of this last movement of the poem with the shape of the first movement, *BN* I. Each movement revolves around an isolated symbolic sentence whose meaning and function may be compositely defined, as we shall note later. See p. 179.) Thus the rightness of a sentence, a phrase, or a single word, will be determined by whether it is 'at home' (*LG* 217) in its context (as *we* were in *BN* I and shall be at the end of *LG* V), playing its part effectively and smoothly in the total dance of utterance, neither weakly redundant nor jarringly obtrusive ('neither diffident nor ostentatious', *LG* 219). Goodness in style is not essentially different from goodness in morality or in social relationships. The old and the new words (like the old and the young, like the traditional and the revolutionary) must work easily together. The plain words (like the world's labourers?) must fulfil their limited and clearly definable function 'without vulgarity' (*LG* 221), and the formal word (like the world's officers and dignitaries) must be properly precise without offensive pedantry, so that the whole poem (like the ideal society, implicitly imaged in *The Idea of a Christian Society, Notes towards the definition of Culture*, and elsewhere in the poet's work) will be as harmoniously whole as a patterned dance or a piece of music. (We scarcely need to refer to the poem's recurring theme of exclusion from music and dancing in order to note how far off this ideal condition is.) When Eliot reiterates, 'Every phrase and every sentence is an end and a beginning' (*LG* 224) one cannot but be conscious of the way in which each 'figure' in a dance is marked off by a change of movement or of partners which is both end and beginning; but it is equally important that every articulate utterance which is the 'end' or outcome of the need to express oneself is also the 'beginning' of communication. (In view of what follows in the allusions to deaths by execution in *LG* 226, the reader will eventually sense that 'sentence' in *LG* 224 carries the further connotation of a judicial sentence.) For the poet each utterance achieved is 'an epitaph' (*LG* 225), both in the sense that it testifies to what was a living experience, which is now past, and in the sense that every attempt in poetry is a failure because 'one has only learnt to get the better of words/For the thing one no longer has to say' (*EC* 176–7).

The theme is pursued in relation to active life. Every action is a move nearer to our death, whether it be the heroic death of execution (like King Charles's), fire (immolation like Heracles's, Dido's and many more, martyrdoms at the stake, wartime deaths in the blitz, and the tragic ends of all who have been trapped by the 'fire or fire' dilemma – all these are no doubt intended), drowning at sea, or the more common lot of the forgotten dead illegibly recorded on our churchyard tombstones (and the even more distantly forgotten dead recorded on 'old stones that cannot be deciphered', *EC* 196). 'That is where we start' (*LG* 227). We must start by facing this truth, that all our actions take us nearer to death; in short, that death is our end.

That 'we die with the dying' (*LG* 228) is true not only in our relationship to those whose physical deaths we attend to, but also in our relationship to those who are dying all around us (cf. *LG* 180) whether in the sense that we and they are dying spiritually through our failure to die to self in obedience to the 'dying nurse' (*EC* 153), or are dying to sin and self, and thereby achieving re-birth. (In the latter case, we, with them, are 'born', *LG* 230 – or re-born, and 'return', *LG* 231.) Thus too we are 'born with the dead' (*LG* 230) whose physical or spiritual deaths we match or accompany. In accompanying them we bear their corpses on our shoulders and are borne away with them. 'We go with them' (*LG* 229) reiterates 'And we all go with them' (*EC* 110), reminding us that the funeral may be 'Nobody's funeral' (*EC* 111) in that the dead (and the mourners too) may have ceased to live long before they died. Lastly, the dead 'return' in the way already enacted in the encounter with the compound ghost of Movement II. The echo of Ezra Pound's poem, *The Return* in the phrase 'See, they return' (*LG* 231) would seem by hindsight to involve Pound in the composite ghost. The fact that Pound was far from dead at the time of composition of this poem would not, I think, prevent Eliot from involving him in this allusive way among the masters to whom he felt deeply indebted.

In all that we do the patterned paradox of conjoint death and birth is worked out: in all our experiences the same principle confronts us. We know ourselves involved as we see others die, for, as Donne said, 'any man's death diminishes me'. But, as experience at Little Gidding (and in London after the air-raid too) testifies, the dead are restored, and the re-birth of their love and insight involve us too. (We recover their discoveries. The poem itself is evidence of this.) The moment of affirmative revelation in the flesh (in natural delight), and the moment of voluntary or involuntary resignation of the flesh (in death) are 'of equal duration' (*LG* 233). Joy in the natural world (of which every instance is a birth) and the discipline of self-surrender (of which every instance is a death) are harmoniously related in the reconciliation which is the key to the whole poem. The past therefore is not a fettering factor, for the philosophy of successiveness which would make it so has been rejected. To be 'without history' (*LG* 233) is not to be 'redeemed' from the compulsive drive of temporal successiveness, for history, truly understood, forms a pattern, not a straight line.

(From *LG* 231, 'See, they return', look back to *LG* 163, 'See, now they vanish', and then to the vanishing acts recorded in *EC* 99–100.) So in any given age history is the given timeless moment, such as the given present now, in a village church in England.

Before leaving this passage we may well take a further look at the pregnant phrase 'Every poem an epitaph' (*LG* 225) because it brings to an end the reflections on poetry which have formed a substantial and important part of the total content of *Four Quartets*. We may say that the problem of poetic craftsmanship and communication has been a speciality of the poem, but we must be careful not to miss its deep and unfailing interconnectedness with all other major themes. The interconnectedness is neatly stressed in the end statement that a poem is an epitaph (as the poet himself is an 'Epitaph' in Donne's *Nocturnal upon St Lucy's Day*), which is true in the sense that the individual personality of the poet 'dies' in the self-sacrificial act of transmuting gathered experience into utterance: the poet's being submits (as the Virgin Mary submitted, with the 'barely prayable Prayer' of *DS* 83–4, 'Be it unto me according to thy word') and the word is indeed brought to life. (We may now recall that even to achieve communication with the compound ghost of the poetic masters, the poet had to submerge his individual personality, become 'intimate' by ceasing to be identifiable in order to match the master's anonymity, *LG* 95–9. He had to communicate with the collective dead in the voice of one whose personality had accepted a voluntary death.)

We are at grips here with a cluster of paradoxes which has been at the heart of Eliot's thinking from the days of *The Waste Land*. It combines many thematic strands, some of which are strong in one poem, some in another, but all of which are ultimately relevant at every point at which an overtone lightly or loudly rings with echoes from any one of them. This thematic cluster, gathered around the Birth/Death paradox, is plainly brought to life in *The Journey of the*

Magi for instance, where it is explored primarily in terms of power (the kingdoms of this world): but that is *one* thematic treatment only. The cluster is in no sense Eliot's special property or invention, so that we may justly sum its significance up in general terms.

The earth dies in winter to be reborn in spring; it submits to the wound of the plough and to impregnation by the seed and becomes thus fruitful. A woman dies in commitment of herself to a man: she submits to the wounding of the sex act and becomes thus fruitful. Man dies in commitment of himself to the divine incursion which is a spiritual impregnation by the living word, the divine seed, and thus becomes a partner in the work of the creative God. Man's dread of cruel spring and his reluctance to respond to the supernatural demand of the tiger-like Christ must be seen in terms of this parallelism. It is comparable to woman's ambiguous response to man's threat of sexual invasion. Man wants and does not want to escape from the false comforts and distracting distractions of living and partly living. What we have called woman's conjoint No/Yes (with which the choruses of *Murder in the Cathedral* continually resound) expresses a parallel reluctance to submit the self to the death and pain from which creation springs. Thomas the martyr faces the universal human situation sharpened to a point of maximum intensity. In order to make the required correspondences Eliot necessarily made the Chorus of *Murder in the Cathedral* a female one. (A central theme of Joyce's *Ulysses* is the progress from Molly Bloom's first utterance 'Mn', to her final 'Yes'.)

We take up here the sexual theme in the Birth/Death cluster precisely because Eliot does not seem to have made a great deal of it in *Four Quartets* (though there may well be more than has yet been recognized). He has rather laid emphasis on the theme of poetic labour and creation, which is fully explored. But the occasional hints of a sexual parallelism in *Four Quartets* (to which we have intermittently drawn attention) have been noted because each such hint points to an element in the fuller presentation of Eliot's synthesis than even his *Four Quartets* provides – and that is the presentation represented by his work as a whole. We may well apply to Eliot's output the judgement which he applied to Shakespeare's – that 'if any one of Shakespeare's plays were omitted we should not be able to understand the rest as well as we do' (*The Use of Poetry and the Use of Criticism*, p. 44).

Four Quartets is no doubt Eliot's maturest and richest imaginative vision. Many constant themes in his thinking are fully articulated here: but there are necessarily others, inextricably related to them, which are lightly touched on here and receive full articulation elsewhere in his work. We must not pretend that what is lightly touched on here is other than lightly touched on. Neither must we ignore it and pretend that it is not present at all, if only because it will have its place in the consummation represented by the coming final passage. That is our justification for noting, before we encounter the consummation, the rich multifariousness of Eliot's reachings-out in the movements that precede it, and for pausing to pick up threads, slender or strong, which are knitted together to produce a comprehensiveness of poetic statement rarely matched in literature.

The texture is rich not only because of the varied yet harmonious thematic outreach, but also because the threads have drawn together into a common pattern the experience of many characters, historical and fictional, with widely differing associations. The superficial unlikeliness of Eliot's ingathering is itself significant: it speaks, we may say, and leave it at that: any attempt to comment upon it would probably cheapen it. The involvement takes in King Charles, Nicholas Ferrar, the Prodigal Son, Tennyson, Shelley, Heracles, Hamlet, Antony, Julian of Norwich, Aeneas, Dante, Brunetto Latini, Maud's Lover, John Donne, Hiawatha and many more of varying degrees of shadowiness or recognizability. And the common pattern of experience in which they are involved is itself a complex of related patterns

articulated on different levels of action, personal, professional, national, civilizational, and racial, with material
woven of the fabric of family, sexual, social, intellectual, and
spiritual life.

Rather than lose ourselves in a maze of explorations and
correspondences, it is better to let Eliot's chosen rhythm of
presentation speak for itself. The conclusion is to give us a
decisive recovery of Dante's beatific vision such as was pre-
echoed in the address to the Virgin Mary in *Dry Salvages* IV,
for that movement, like this one, took us back to the Garden
in which our first glimpse and foretaste of the glory was
granted to us, by establishing the Virgin Mary, herself
traditionally Garden and Fountain, as the obedient Mother
of the Divine, and thereby throwing back upon all that is
natural and human the vocation to serve as Bride of the
Creator and bring forth the Son of God. This throwback
feeds into the image of the Flower-bearing pool in the
Garden a rich harmony of associations, theological and
mystical, sexual and romantic.

With the drawing of this Love and the voice of this Calling

This is a quotation from *The Cloud of Unknowing*. Its very in-
clusion, calling up the unspoken title of the medieval work
of mysticism, gives a richer connotation to all previous
usages of the word 'cloud' and indeed to the whole complex
theme of darkness and dust. The connotative enrichment
here effected was referred to in advance in our commentary
on *LG* II (see p. 136). The *revelation* and the *demand* have been
the two modes of divine communication with man recurring
throughout the poem; the drawing and the calling. The
revelation – such as the moment in the rose-garden – draws
us. The demand or, we may say, the vocation – whether to
work, prayer, discipline, or other form of self-surrender – is
equally the expression of God's love. The 'drawing' is not
necessarily affirmative and joyful: the 'voice' does not necessarily call to what is costly and sacrificial. Either may be
either affirmative or negative. Both will be both. For God's

love *draws* us too in devising 'torment' (*LG* 207) and it *calls* us as well in the voices in the garden. Within the concepts *drawing* and *calling*, the pattern of the divine Love's momentous dealings with us can be fitly summed up.

Like the first movement of *Burnt Norton* this final movement is a sequence of two phases, speculative exploration and concrete imaginative experience, which revolves around a central sentence. The symbolic similarity of the two central sentences (*BN* 15–17 and *LG* 238) is important, for the probing finger, questioning our memories (*BN* 16) or questioning our wounds (*EC* 147–8), belongs to the 'bleeding hands' (*EC* 149) and 'the hands that wove' (*LG* 209), and behind the hands that wove is the 'unfamiliar Name' (*LG* 208), Love, now plainly drawing. The darkness in *The Hound of Heaven* turned out to be, after all, 'shade of his Hand outstretched caressingly', and here too, in conclusion 'menace and caress' (*DS* 29) turn out to be one and the same. For if all pointing and probing fingers are implicitly linked, all voices become as one Voice, whether the voice of music or of yelping monster, whether bird voices or sea voices, whether hidden laughter or the soundless wailing of suffering. From the packed world opened up in *Four Quartets* there is now an immense accumulation of remembered illuminations that draw us, and a great volume of calling voices is about our ears. (Cloud of Unknowing or Cloud of Witnesses?) There is no punctuation at the end of this crucial line: for it is within the compass of the drawing and in hearing of the voice that what follows follows.

We shall not cease from exploration

Just as he earlier found a place for sin (*LG* 166), so now Eliot works into his scheme ultimately something of the posture of forward-looking progressiveness characteristic of the humanistic liberalism which has been so much under attack; for unending human 'exploration' has its proper place in the pattern, provided that we realize that all our exploring leads, not forward on a straight line, but round

and back to our starting-point. For our true 'end' is to realize
the true character of our beginning – to get to know the
divine origin of ourselves and our world, the real nature of
that goodness and joy from whose full enjoyment our birth
(in its deathlikeness) and our fall have temporally (and
temporarily) excluded us. Because of this human and
terrestrial exclusion, based on the limitation of temporality
and the fact of sin, our only progress has to be through a
'gate' (*LG* 243) – a barrier 'unknown' to us in our usual
time-locked, desire-ridden thinking and acting, but 'remembered' in our moments of revelatory joy and suffering.
We ourselves, reading this poem, became again dimly aware
of the gate through sharing in the suffering of another (*DS*
108–9), and that other the lover of *Maud* (*EC* 49) and the
many other sufferers from exclusion with whom he is implicitly associated by the poem.

Thus we have been through the crucial cycle in our own
reading. It was after our sharing the suffering of the poet –
and of all those whose agony his agony reflected and whose
agony he sufferingly observed (*DS* II) that we came to the
foot of the Cross in sharing the pain of waiting women 'who
have seen their sons or husbands/Setting forth, and not
returning' (*DS* 175–6). There we found ourselves in the
company of the Virgin Mother, model alike of the painful
obedience demanded of us and of the joyful vocation offered
us. Then, looking back, we understood the meaning of the
revelation in the Garden of childhood innocence, personal
and primeval. Then too, looking forward (if we *could* have
looked forward), we should have understood the character
of the recovery to which our prayerful acceptance and penitence would lead us.

That is 'where we start', the poet said above (*LG* 227) of
the realization of the suffering and death involved in every
action, every creation, every birth, noting that even a poem
is an epitaph. And the end we achieve is to return in full
understanding to the place where 'we started' (*LG* 240), this
time knowing it for what it is, the lost Eden, yet the Eden

recovered, the past glimpses of joy and illumination scattered over our lives, yet the future and present heaven opened up to view in the beatific vision granted to Dante by the 'Queen of Heaven' (*DS* 178) into whose pattern of suffering and action we have entered, by sharing the annunciations, painful and joyful, to become ourselves possible vehicles for the birth of the divine within the human and the natural.

'Where we started' (*LG* 240) is a pregnant phrase. For our racial and spiritual origins were in the garden, as indeed were our childhood beginnings. But 'we started' our experience of reading the poem there too, for that was where the poet first took us. And 'we started' in another sense – *were startled* – by the revelation given to us (where Eve 'started' also: see p. 14). Moreover, we may now add also that the poet's probing finger, disturbing our dusty minds (*BN* 15–16), caused us to 'start' too, as he called us into the cycle of movement through death to birth, through descent to ascent. (cf. 'Home is where one starts from', *EC* 190.)

The only true progress open to us, then, is the progress in humanity and wisdom, which means in humility and self-surrender, and it will lead us to that penultimate stage at which there remains nothing else on earth for us to 'discover' (*LG* 244) except that which constituted 'the beginning' of all our search and effort, the recurring glimpses of our paradisal origins (and heavenly 'end'), in this poem symbolized in the images of the hidden waterfall, the voices, the laughter, the children, and everything clustered about them in the Garden which contained them and brought them forth.

The pattern of Eliot's poem is again proved to be in perfect harmony with the pattern of his thinking; for we now return as readers to the garden of *Burnt Norton* and fully recognize what it is for the first time. The syllable 'fall' in 'Waterfall' (cf. 'nightfall' and 'smokefall') and 'footfall', and the revelation that the children are in an 'apple-tree' have distinct paradisal associations. Though the 'longest river' of

LG 246 is the river of time, of human history (as in *The Dry Salvages*), it is no doubt also more especially associated with the Mississippi, the world's longest river, whose source is in the state of Minnesota. Here again then, 'at the source of the longest river' (*LG* 246), we are in the territory of the Dacotahs, and it is impossible not to hear the voice of Minnehaha in 'the voice of the hidden waterfall' (*LG* 247), calling to the youthful Hiawatha on his journey to fetch his bride. (Longfellow's own note on 'Minnehaha' puts the matter beyond dispute: 'Laughing Water; a waterfall on a stream running into the Mississippi between Fort Snelling and the Falls of St Antony.') And now we must observe, in greater detail, how the image of the children takes us back to *New Hampshire*, the first of the short lyrics, *Landscapes* (1934–5) –

> 'Children's voices in the orchard
> Between the blossom – and the fruit-time'

and the voice of the darting bird to *Cape Ann* (the Cape which gives us the coastal setting of *The Dry Salvages*), the fifth and last of the *Landscapes*

> 'O quick quick, quick hear the song-sparrow
> Swamp-sparrow, fox-sparrow, vesper-sparrow
> At dawn and dusk',

where the little bird-sequence (song-, swamp-, fox-, vesper-) offered us a miniature harmony of echoes from the four elements (air, water, earth, fire); after which we were invited to 'Follow the dance . . .'. One does not know whether to be more surprised at the prophetic touch in *Cape Ann* which thus anticipates *Four Quartets*, or at the comprehensiveness of Eliot's backward glances in the last movement of *Little Gidding*.

Thus the moments of revelation or half-revelation, in which the voices of unfallen man and innocent nature have been heard, patterned together, constitute, for the poet in his living experience, and for the reader in his poetic experience, the meaning – the meaning which was in the beginning. The revelations were given when they were not being 'looked for' (*LG* 249) and the full recovery of them likewise demands a condition of self-unconcern, 'of complete simplicity' (*LG* 253), that purity of heart which costs everything. The final and total recovery and reconciliation is symbolized in the uniting of images, fire and rose, supernatural and natural, divine and human, sacrificial and sacramental – for the tongues of flame are folded in upon themselves and tied together in the form of a rose.

Since the first appearance of the flower in the garden, the rose has gathered significance, and has become a rich affirmative symbol of love and beauty and order, offered and tasted at the earthly level, through its sexual, religious, and monarchical associations. Much of the significance has been added obliquely in that Eliot's allusions to Dante have inevitably enriched the meaning of the rose, as they have involved the reader in recollection of a poetic statement which powerfully reinforces Eliot's own exploration of the Affirmative Way. At the conclusion of the *Divine Comedy* Dante is granted the vision of Heaven in which the hosts of the blessed are gathered together in the form of a pure white rose (*Paradiso* XXXI, 1 ff.). Eliot's last images, prefaced by a triumphant reiteration of Julian of Norwich's declaration that 'all shall be well' (*LG* 255), form themselves a closely-knit, flower-like cluster, resounding with overtones from earlier in the poem and even introducing some new ones. For the tying-up of the tongues of fire gathers together the apostolic tongues of flame with the flames from pyre and pyre, of martyrs and lovers, saints and suicides, men burnt up with spiritual devotion and men burnt up with passion. The word 'in-folded' (*LG* 257) carries overtones of the leaves of a book bound in a volume, and thus reminds us that 'the communication/Of the dead', to which we are now attending as we read *Four Quartets*, 'is tongued with fire beyond the language of the living' (*LG* 50–1). To this cluster of overtones must be added those of the sheepfold into which sheep lost and found are all in-folded.

We should miss the full significance of the final ingathering if we did not sense how careful Eliot has been to make it, on the Dantean pattern, a clustering of people, not just of ideas. 'Find them', we were told in *BN* I (19), and we went off in pursuit of echoes. We found people, real and fictional. The gathered *'tongues* of flame' (*LG* 257) are gathered voices – the voices we have heard and recognized, and those we have yet to identify – apostles and poets, saints and sinners, and a vast ancestry, cultural and personal, which moved briefly before our eyes in the phantasmagoric encounter in *LG* II.

The 'crowned knot of fire' (*LG* 258) thus formed is especially representative of the human and the divine jointly exalted, for while the word 'knot' carries overtones drawn from its use in descriptions of the Trinity (Donne speaks of Christ's 'jointure in the knotty Trinity' in *Holy Sonnets* XVI), it also carries overtones for readers of Donne's *The Ecstasy* (already echoed in *BN* 28) of the knitting together of the physical and the spiritual characteristic of our humanity ('That subtle knot that makes us man').

The identification of clustered flames with clustered rose-leaves magnificently unifies the rich tensions of known Christian paradox, but Eliot's harmonics overarch the cadence with a music that intellect cannot reach. For the final reconciliation seems to draw together all opposites of which human experience is painfully and joyfully compounded, yet without conceding a syllable to sentimentality or imprecision; and that in itself is a miracle.

Appendix I

BURNT NORTON, MOVEMENT II

Garlic and sapphires in the mud . . .

The difficulties of this passage are notorious. No one who is acquainted with Eliot's practice of multiplying allusions on the personal, historical, literary, and religious levels, can suppose that justice has yet been done to it. We are teased by the provocative mystery of the images into explorations which have, inevitably, a highly conjectural status. We are justified in making them by the fact that they may stimulate thinking which will eventually produce interpretation that is valid and sure.

This said, we suggest that to explore the full significance of the possible sexual reference in this passage, we might look forward to the three crucial lines later in this movement, *BN* 85–7:

> 'But only in time can the moment in the rose-garden,
> The moment in the arbour where the rain beat,
> The moment in the draughty church at smokefall
> Be remembered. . . .'

These lines seem to refer to a series of revelatory moments at once personal and universal. The first, the 'moment in the rose-garden', takes us back to *Burnt Norton* I. The third takes us on to *Little Gidding*. But the second, 'the moment in the arbour where the rain beat', does not appear to refer to any moment recorded within *Four Quartets* unless it be to this passage opening *BN* II. It is tempting, therefore, to make a case that the experience of the 'dance along the artery' and the ascent 'to summer in the tree' is a particular moment of delight that occurred in the arbour, which alongside its personal autobiographical memories carries too its archetypal associations.

The tentative suggestion may be hazarded that in this case the archetypal associations are perhaps rooted in Virgil's *Aeneid* and that we may have an allusion here to Aeneas's act of love with Dido when the two take shelter from the sudden storm which interrupts the boar-hunt. With this correspondence in mind (and there is yet other material which might be said to corroborate it) we should find the images of the passage powerfully enriched in meaning and, what is more important, given a coherence and inevitability otherwise difficult to establish. Whether the hunt would include a vehicle whose crude axle might have become embedded in the mud is a question which one must leave to the experts. The image is so suggestive otherwise that our reading does not depend on that assumption. The 'inveterate scars' and the forgotten wars carry possible Virgilian overtones, and that the harmony of the union between Aeneas and Dido should be 'figured in the drift of stars', while the pattern of pursuit between hunter and hunted is 'reconciled among the stars', reminds us that Venus and Juno jointly arranged the coming together. The 'light upon the figured leaf', could be, in its external sense, produced by a flash of lightning, forerunner of the 'winter lightning' (*DS* 209) experienced when the earth is once more 'sodden' (*LG* 2).

The distinctly conjectural status of these readings is self-evident. The justification for hazarding them at all is twofold. In the first place they enable the reader of *Four Quartets* to give to the teasing line

'The moment in the arbour where the rain beat' (*BN* 86)

something of the highly charged significance which its placing seems to demand. In the second place, as other critics have pointed out, there are several points of the poem at which the allusive vocabulary recalls the *Aeneid*, hinting at correspondences such as the one now proposed. In *Little Gidding* it becomes evident that the theme of Dido's self-immolation for love of Aeneas is deeply planted in Eliot's thinking:

> 'The only hope, or else despair
> Lies in the choice of pyre or pyre
> To be redeemed from fire by fire.' (*LG* 204–6)

Moreover the poet's meeting with the compound ghost in *Little Gidding* recalls Aeneas's meeting with Palinurus in the underworld.

There can be no doubt about the immense significance of Virgil for Eliot. In his essay, *What is a Classic?* Eliot speaks of Virgil as having for all Europe 'the centrality of the unique classic'. Virgil's comprehensiveness and universality provide Eliot with a literary and cultural standard over against which he is ready to use the word 'provincial'. And there is in Eliot an unmistakable tendency to identify himself (not pompously, but simply as struggling man) with the figure of Aeneas.

> 'Aeneas is himself, from first to last, a 'man in fate', a man who is neither an adventurer nor a careerist, a man fulfilling his destiny, not under compulsion or arbitrary decree, and certainly from no stimulus to glory, but by surrendering his will to a higher power behind the gods who would thwart or direct him. He would have preferred to stop in Troy, but he becomes an exile, and something greater and more significant than any exile; he is exiled for a purpose greater than he can know, but which he recognizes; and he is not, in a human sense, a happy or successful man.' (*What is a Classic?* p. 28)

And later:

> 'I have spoken of the new seriousness – *gravity* I might say – the new insight into history, illustrated by the dedication of Aeneas to Rome, to a future far beyond his living achievement. *His* reward was hardly more than a narrow beach-head and a political marriage in a weary middle age; his youth interred, its shadow moving with the shades the other side of Cumae.' (*What is a Classic?* p. 32)

In connection with Eliot's tendency to identify himself with Aeneas one should mention that in his notes to *The Waste Land* he is at pains to press the reference to St Augustine's *Confessions* intended in the highly charged line –

'To Carthage then I came'.

and does not add that Aeneas too came to Carthage, to be embroiled in a tragic love. But it must be remembered that reference to St Augustine *includes* reference to Virgil for anyone familiar with the *Confessions*. For St Augustine himself Virgil's powerful account of the love of Aeneas for Dido is representative of earthly interests and passions which distract the cultured mind from full surrender to God.

> 'For what more miserable than a miserable being who commiserates not himself; weeping the death of Dido for love to Aeneas, but weeping not his own death for want of love to Thee, O God'.   *(Confessions,* I, xii.)

And of course Eliot's focusing of attentions upon St Augustine exclusively may well represent one of the numerous instances of putting into practice his chosen motto, *tace et fac*. Certainly the acceptance of allusion to *Aeneid* IV as well as to St Augustine's *Confessions* in *The Fire Sermon*, 307, obviously adds significance to the succeeding lines:

> 'Burning burning burning burning
> O Lord Thou pluckest me out' (308–9),

lines which it is impossible for the reader immersed in Eliot to dissociate from the choice of 'pyre or pyre', 'fire or fire' offered in *Little Gidding*.

We are not suggesting that Eliot's adoption of Virgil's *Aeneid* as an archetypal framework to sustain occasional allusions embodied in poetic overtones is a predominant element in the poem's construction. The overall pattern of the *Quartets* contains allusive correspondences with constructs as diverse as *In Memoriam, The Divine Comedy*, and the parable of The Prodigal Son. In this respect, as in so many others, Eliot learned from Joyce who, in different ways, and in different degrees used the *Odyssey*, *Hamlet*, and the *Divine Comedy* as archetypal frameworks in constructing *Ulysses* and in thickening its allusive texture. Perhaps Joyce's networks of correspondences are fuller and more systematic than anything Eliot attempted, but the similarity is sharper than has been allowed for.

In this connection it is perhaps noteworthy that the Irish nationalists in *Ulysses* press the theme that the Irish are the spiritual heirs of the Greeks and the English the heirs of the Romans. There is a good deal of mockery of English civilization as being, like the Roman, a materialistic one, more prolific of water-closets than of poetry. That Eliot should accept the Roman identification for English culture and take up the Virgilian identification in his own persona as poet is apt and comprehensible. The mutual recognition between Joyce and Eliot of their proper literary stature is not open to question. The interest of the two writers in each other's technique of verbal allusion is evident. These points are worth mentioning here if only because the archetypal significance of the boar-hunt (*BN* 59) in the life of the poet has special dimensions for the Joycean who is familiar with the *Scylla and Charybdis* episode in *Ulysses*. It is a significance which in Joyce relates essentially to the sex life of the compound artist, Shakespeare–Stephen Dedalus, and goes back in origin to the personal Shakespearean revelation assumed to have been made in *Venus and Adonis*. (The involvement of Venus again fills out the network of correspondences further.)

Appendix II

FOUR QUARTETS AND *HIAWATHA*

We have noted that 'The voice of the hidden waterfall'
(*LG* 247) and the recurring image of laughter behind trees
cannot be disentangled, for the reader of Longfellow, from
the memory of Minnehaha, Laughing Water, whose laughter
is heard calling to Hiawatha through the silence – the call
that brings him to his bride and to happiness. (See *Hiawatha*
X, *Hiawatha's Wooing*.) Moreover, an underlying theme of
Hiawatha is man's gradual conquest of Nature in the world
around him, and the corresponding disciplining of himself by
struggle, trial, and fasting. Forces of air and fire, earth and
water, are the contestants confronting Hiawatha in his
arduous pilgrimage. Another possible connection concerns
the line

'The moment in the arbour where the rain beat' (*BN* 86)

which has already been discussed in Appendix I but which,
no doubt, must continue to tease the reader of *Four Quartets*.
In the first place, one asks why *where* instead of *when*, which
would surely be the more natural word. In the second place,
the phrase 'rain beat' has an awkward ring – as though its
usage were contrived in order to produce a significant echo
or ambiguity. Consequently I have wondered whether the
line might have been designed to carry a secondary reference to a rain-bird (wood-pecker) beating a tree. There is an
important 'moment' in *Hiawatha* when a woodpecker brings
a message to the weary hero, resting at a time of crisis among
the pine trees. Mama, the woodpecker, instructs Hiawatha
to aim his arrows at the head of Megissogwon (*Hiawatha* IX,

Hiawatha and the Pearl Feather). This is worth noting because the 'death of earth' (*LG* 69), imaged by the corpse half in the sea, half on the sand, recalls the dead Megissogwon –

> 'On the shore he left the body,
> Half on land and half in water,
> In the sand his feet were buried,
> And his face was in the water' –

killed by Hiawatha under Mama's instruction.

We now turn again to the difficult opening of *Burnt Norton* II, and first to the line 'Garlic and sapphires in the mud'. It is worth saying that the identifiable *locale* of *Four Quartets* seems to be chiefly in England or the U.S.A. If one were to ask where sapphires might in fact be found in the mud, the answer would be that the sapphire-producing area of the U.S.A. is the state of Montana, the territory of the Indians, at the base of the Rockies. One would not wish to make much of a reference by Longfellow to the baby Hiawatha 'Bedded soft in moss and rushes' (cf. *BN* 48) even though it is succeeded by a picture of the stars ('the Death-Dance of the spirits', 'the broad white road in heaven/Pathway of the ghosts') which reads interestingly alongside *BN* 53–5, but one must consider seriously the possibility that the 'bedded axle-tree' (*BN* 48) may carry the connotation of the centre-pole of a wigwam.

In *Hiawatha* XII, *The Son of the Evening Star*, we are told a story whose basis is the theme of time sequence deranged by the experience of young manhood's summer in age's winter. The theme itself touches the nerve of Eliot's reader. Owenee, the youngest of a hunter's daughters, laughingly rejects all her lovers while her nine sisters marry young and handsome suitors, and then marries Osseo, son of the Evening Star, now aged and ugly. Now it is Owenee's turn to be mocked. Old Osseo prays miserably to the Star of Evening and is transformed from the winter of old age to the summer of youth, only to find that Owenee has been correspondingly transformed from youth to age. Sitting down at a family feast in the wigwam, Osseo hears a voice calling him –

> 'Come to me: *ascend*, Osseo . . . (cf. *BN* 55)
> What Osseo heard as whispers,
> What as words he comprehended,
> Was but music to the others
> Music as of birds afar off . . .'

Then occurs the remarkable event –

> 'Then the lodge began to tremble,
> Straight began to shake and tremble,
> And they felt it rising, rising,
> Slowly through the air ascending . . .
> Till it passed the topmost branches' (cf. *BN* 55–6).

Mocking sisters and husbands are now changed into birds while Owenee is restored to youth and beauty. The wigwam makes a further ascent –

> 'And amid celestial splendours
> On the Evening Star alighted.'

It is difficult to forget this story of a wigwam rising to a perch among the treetops, then to a perch among the stars, when one is reading *BN* 55–61. Moreover, *Four Quartets* is a poem in which parallels between the body of man and the body which is his world recur (cf. *EC* II) and thus the 'inveterate scars' of *BN* 50 might refer especially to the Rocky Mountains as well as to the surface of the human body, and link thus with the reference to the American desert in *LG* 66 ff. Likewise the 'long-forgotten wars' (*BN* 51) would refer to the world's geological history as well as to man's chronicled history, and would put overtones of the struggle against the Indians alongside overtones of the American Civil War in the allusions to American history in particular. Corroboration for such a view would be provided by the argument that an allusion to the calumet, the pipe of peace, is faintly implicit in *LG* 54. (See how the old men receive the Paleface missionaries in *Hiawatha* XXII.)

Appendix III

MORE HIDDEN MUSIC

1. *BN* 149–52. These lines contain a concealed allusion to Christ (the Word) stumbling under the weight of the cross. The evidence is, firstly the ubiquitous correspondence between *word* and *Word*, and the special, metrically emphatic link between 'Words' (*BN* 149) and 'The Word' (*BN* 155); and secondly that 'slide' (*BN* 151) pre-echoes 'narrowing rails slide together' (*DS* 141), thereby calling up the phrase 'left that station' (*DS* 139), while 'station' echoes 'stops too long between stations' (*EC* 118). The unspoken word, *Stations of the Cross* (the Virgin Mary and other sorrowful women are keeping their station there, *DS* 175) helps to tie this little cluster of associations into a knot. The *Stations* is another ceremony marked by bells. (It may well follow that the narrowing rails sliding together in *DS* 141 are sanctuary rails too. The line is a packed one: see App. III, 4.) Jesus falls under the weight of the cross at three of the *Stations*. Follow this treasure-hunt farther (holding all the threads together, and noting again *DS* 175–6) and you may see women during the First World War standing and waving on a station platform as their departing sons are lost behind a cloud of steam (*BN* 128).

2. *EC* 172–83 and *EC* V generally. Here are hidden allusive references to Elizabethan history. The 'middle way' (*EC* 172) no doubt hints at the *via media* of the Elizabethan religious settlement. The vocabulary of verbal warfare ('venture', 'raid', 'shabby equipment', 'undisciplined squads' – *EC* 178–82) recalls the hit-and-run tactics employed against Spanish

vessels. The emphasis on discovery corroborates the case. Among the many shadowy presences thus added to the poem we should no doubt include Cranmer (his 'lifetime burning in every moment', *EC* 194, for his voice has been heard in the *Prayer Book* echoes) and other martyrs at the stake, who will later join with Mary Queen of Scots and the venturers at the gathering implicit in *LG* 225–7: 'And any action | Is a step to the block, to the fire, down the sea's throat'.

3. *DS* 26–48. Conjoint images of birth and death haunt this passage, in which suffering women, lying in bed, are plainly present (*DS* 39 ff.). The words 'breaks' and 'water', the grinding of teeth, and the 'wailing warning from the approaching head—' (*DS* 29–31) may well take the sensitive reader's mind into the labour ward. The 'heaving groaner | Rounded homewards' (*DS* 32–3) certainly seems to allude both to a woman 'heaving to parturition' (*Murder in the Cathedral*, p. 43) and the making of a home, as well as to a dying person (to 'the agony in the curtained bedroom, whether of birth or of dying', *The Family Reunion*, p. 96).

4. *DS* 132–52. Numerous scattered overtones, when gathered together, relate these travellers and voyagers with those who were lost in the sinking of the *Titanic* and in the Tay Bridge disaster. Follow the trail of associations from *DS* 179–80 to *DS* 142 and then to the radio call 'at nightfall, in the rigging and the aerial', tapped out in morse, 'not to the ear . . . and not in any language' (*DS* 147–8). Note that the reiterated 'future' (*DS* 138 and 145) echoes *DS* 71 and calls up the 'ocean littered with wastage' (*DS* 70) and the 'drifting wreckage' (*DS* 82). Observe that the psalmist's 'They that go down to the sea in ships' (cf. our comment on *DS* 170–1, p. 110) may be linked with *EC* 62, 'Until the Sun and Moon go down' (the fall of the Titans, the Sun, and Moon), note the reign of 'the ice-cap' (*EC* 67) and the allusion to the *Titanic* is established. Relate *EC* 62 to the hymn, *Nearer, my God, to Thee* ('Though, like the wanderer, | The

sun gone down, Darkness comes over me . . .'), which was sung by the passengers at the last, and then listen to the almost unbearable harmonics of 'music heard so deeply | That it is not heard at all, but you are the music | While the music lasts' (*DS* 210–12), and of 'The chill ascends from feet to knees' (*EC* 162).

The advice given in *DS* 137–8 and 144–5 applies to the travellers by train as well as to the voyagers and calls up by echo the same imagery of the sea littered with wastage and wreckage in relation to their journey too. Note how the granite coast (*DS* 30), the dark lake (*LG* 37) and the reported appearances of a sea monster (*DS* 185) suggest Scotland. Overtones left by the 'problem confronting the builder of bridges' (*DS* 5) and the subsequent reminder that the river remains 'implacable' and a 'destroyer' (*DS* 7–8) should be borne in mind. Then read *DS* 141 ('While the narrowing rails slide together behind you') alongside the echoed phrase, 'Under the tension, slip, slide, perish' (*BN* 151) and remember how 'the North East lowers | Over shallow banks unchanging and erosionless' (*DS* 74–5). Finally, note that the Tay is the longest river in Scotland. The 'voice of the hidden waterfall' | 'At the source of the longest river' (*LG* 246–7) can certainly refer to Tummel Falls ('tumble' of course) at the source of the Tay, as well as to Laughing Water. (There is Tummel Bridge too.) The voice of this Fall is indeed half-heard in the strange use of 'tumble down' (*EC* 56) just before the reference to the Titanic Fall (*EC* 62). 'Red into grey' (*EC* 56) is the Macduff tartan of the Earls of Fife. Not only does it help to place the Tay Bridge; it calls up memories of Duncan, Malcolm, and Macbeth to strengthen the immediate theme of rebellion (*EC* 51–67) and the later theme of the murdered king.

5. *LG* 19–20. 'Where is the summer?' The question has already been answered in *BN* 55, 'Ascend to summer in the tree'. This is one of a number of lines in unpunctuated sections of the poem which have a syntactical ambiguity.

(These difficult sections are themselves the 'distempered' parts of the poem for they record the violent ups and downs of the poet's fever chart. As such they need to be *questioned*. See *EC* 148.) Read *BN* 55 as an imperative, then, and it answers the question put in *LG* 19–20. Read it thus along-side *EC* 151, 'resolving the enigma of the fever chart' (which *LG* 20 calls up: see p. 126), and the 'tree' is clearly the Cross on to which the Christian must be lifted up in order to taste the summer which is 'not in time's covenant' (*LG* 14). So lifted up (because the tree is also the tree in the garden), he will be able to see what the children can see and fully understand what previously has been 'but heard, half-heard' (*LG* 250) – all those overtones of the poem which constitute its hidden treasure. The treasure is the Word un-spoken. Lifted up into the 'unimaginable summer', 'not in time's covenant', one is lifted both out of servitude to time's successiveness and, as reader of the poem, out of the pursuit of meaning-in-successiveness. One sees the 'light upon the figured leaf': one understands the poem's figurative allusive-ness; while the 'boarhound and the boar' (the bore, I suspect) pursue *their* pattern, trying to read it in the same progressive way as they vainly try to read life itself.

Index

Acts of the Apostles, 132

Adam, 14, 68–9, 72, 83, 162

Aeneas, 25, 50, 100, 155, 158, 169, 177, 186–8

Aeneid (Virgil), 20, 50, 76, 154, 158, 186

Affirmation, Way of, 11, 14, 26, 30–1, 39, 71, 104

America, 9 n., 20, 79, 83, 100, 138, 161, 191

Ancient Mariner, The (Coleridge), 144

Andrea del Sarto (Browning), 14, 114

Angelus, 10, 32, 92, 113, 170

Antony and Cleopatra, 157–8, 167, 169, 177

Ascent of Mount Carmel, 65

Ash Wednesday (Eliot), 10, 11, 12, 28, 35, 93, 136–7

Baptism, 139, 171

Barnes, Djuna, 159

Beckett, Samuel, 2, 3, 53 n., 142

Bhagavad-Gita, 102

Bloom, Molly, 77, 80, 176

Boston, Mass., 82, 88

Browning, Robert, 17, 114

Brunetto Latini, 147–8, 158, 163, 177

Cape Ann, 82, 88

Cape Ann (Eliot), 83, 182

Charles I, King, 4, 123–4, 128, 134, 162, 166, 173, 177

Christ, 13, 32–3, 38, 44, 68–9, 71, 92–3, 110–11, 119–20, 135–6, 142, 150, 162, 167, 171, 176, 193

Church, The, 33, 68, 101, 133, 140, 170, 171

Civil War (American), 20, 83, 113, 192

Civil War (English), 17, 124, 161–4

Cloud of Unknowing, 10, 136, 178

Coleridge, S. T., 144

Common Prayer, Book of, 69, 194

Conan Doyle, Sir A., 56

Conrad, Joseph, 13 n.

Coriolanus, 101–2, 168–9

Cranmer, Thomas, 194

Creator, God the, 13, 35, 68, 136, 167

Cromwell, Oliver, 17

Crucifixion, 12, 16, 32, 35, 43, 52, 83, 135, 162–4, 171, 180

Dacotahs, 182

Dans le Restaurant (Eliot), 25

Dante, 14, 20, 29, 56, 72, 73, 76–7, 111, 144–8, 154–5, 158, 178, 181, 183–4, 188–9

Davies, Sir John, 17–18, 28, 39, 45–7, 68–9, 81, 90

Deianira, 168

Dido, 25, 50, 86, 168–9, 173, 186–8

Donne, John, 12, 64, 98, 101, 114, 144, 145, 148, 155, 157, 163, 166, 174–7, 184

Drew, Elizabeth, 42

Dryden, John, 147

Ecstasy, The (Donne), 12, 155, 184

Eden, Garden of, 8, 83, 100, 124, 135, 180

Elijah, 132
Elyot, Sir Thomas, 41–5, 51, 81, 98
Enoch Arden (Tennyson), 18, 145
Eve, 14, 83, 86, 156, 181
Exodus, 132
Ezekiel, 93

Family Reunion, The (Eliot), 194
Felix culpa, 161
Ferrar, Nicholas, 123, 177
Fielding, Henry, 53 n.
Fife, 195
Florence, 14, 114

Gabriel, Archangel, 92
Geoffrey of Monmouth, 51
Gloucester, Mass. (and England), 82–3
Good Friday, Riding Westward (Donne), 101, 114, 144, 163
Grecian Urn, Ode on a (Keats), 119

Hallam, Arthur, 153
Hamlet, 4, 102, 157, 166–9, 177
Hampshire Chronicle, The, 88
Heracles, 168–73, 177
Heraclitus, 140–1
Herbert, George, 123
Hiawatha (Longfellow), 20, 25, 50, 119, 137, 177, 182, 190 ff.
Hollow Men, The (Eliot), 13 n., 49
Holy Sonnets (Donne), 184
Holy Spirit, 11–13, 111, 124, 130, 133, 136, 139, 142, 151, 167, 170
Homer, 73, 189
Hound of Heaven, The, (Thompson) 4, 8, 56 n., 57, 88, 136, 142, 179, 193
Hound of the Baskervilles, The (Conan Doyle), 56–7, 88

Idea of a Christian Society, The (Eliot), 172
Incarnation, 21, 23, 111, 119, 120
Indians, 192
In Memoriam (Tennyson), 18, 34, 49, 153, 155, 188

Journey of the Magi (Eliot), 70–1, 175
Joyce, James, 1, 2, 14, 34, 56 n., 77, 80, 110, 114, 137, 162, 163, 167, 176, 189
Julian of Norwich, 90, 160, 165, 169, 177, 183

Keats, John, 119, 143, 145
Kierkegaard, Søren, 108, 133
King Lear, 144
Krishna, 63, 103, 107

La Belle Dame sans Merci (Keats), 143
Landscapes (Eliot), 182
Laughing Water, 182, 190–1, 195
Laud, Archbishop, 123, 162
Lewis, C. S., 147
London, 26–9, 43, 88, 124, 135, 137, 139, 154, 167, 174
Longfellow, Henry W., 20, 25, 119, 137, 154, 190–2
Lycidas (Milton), 138

Macbeth, 4, 102, 166, 195
Macdonald, George, 71
Macduff, 195
Mary Queen of Scots, 41, 167, 194
Mass, 25–6, 30, 34, 71, 93, 170
Massachusetts, 82–3, 124
Maud (Tennyson), 18–19, 43, 49–50, 145, 177, 180
Milton, John, 14, 59, 70, 73, 76, 98, 138, 144, 145, 147–8, 162
Minnehaha, 182, 190
Mississippi, 79, 182

Montana, 191

Moses, 132

Murder in the Cathedral (Eliot), 10, 22, 24, 30, 62, 85, 90, 101, 103–5, 121, 176, 194

Negation, Way of, 14, 26, 29, 30–1, 71, 104, 123

Nessus, 168–9

New Hampshire (Eliot), 83, 182

New Jerusalem, 14, 114, 131

Nightwood (Djuna Barnes), 159

Nocturnal upon St Lucy's Day (Donne), 175

Nosce Teipsum (Davies), 39, 68

Notes towards the definition of Culture (Eliot), 172

Old Testament, 132, 172

Orchestra (Davies), 17–18, 28, 46–7, 90

Original Sin, 66, 167

Othello, 102

Palinurus, 154, 158

Paradise Lost, 14, 76, 144

Penelope, 85, 90

Pentecost, 133

Poe, Edgar A., 42, 46 n.

Pound, Ezra, 174

Preston, Raymond, 86

Prodigal Son, 49, 124, 145, 151, 153, 177, 188

Prophecies of Merlin, 51

Proust, Marcel, 56, 72

Redemption, 66, 72, 161

Resurrection, 5, 131, 171

Revelation, Book of, 115

Rocky Mountains, 191–2

St Ann, 82

St Augustine, 161, 188

St John Baptist, 167

St John the Evangelist, 30, 152, 170, 172

St John of the Cross, 40, 65

St Louis, Miss., 79, 82, 90, 104, 124

St Luke, 5, 13, 117, 128

St Mary le bow, 10

St Mary the Virgin, *see* Virgin Mary

Samson Agonistes (Milton), 59

Scorpio, 51

Second Coming of Christ, 117

Shakespeare, William, 45, 52, 64, 73, 81, 102, 137, 144, 145, 148, 154, 157, 166–7, 177

Shelley, Percy B., 93, 99, 112, 119, 137, 143, 146–8, 153–4, 177

Sodom and Gomorrah, 80

Spectral Rose, 164

Stars and Stripes, 20

Stations of the Cross, 193

Tay, River, 6, 194–5

Tempest, The, 137

Tennyson, Lord, 18, 34, 43, 49, 88, 145, 153–5, 177, 188

Thompson Francis, 4, 8, 56 n., 136

Times Literary Supplement, The, 142

Titanic, 6, 112, 194–5

To Criticize the Critic (Eliot), 146

Triumph of Life, The (Shelley), 147

Troilus and Cressida, 52

Troy, 100, 187

Tummel Falls (and Bridge), 195

Ulysses (Joyce), 1, 2, 56 n., 77, 80, 85, 110, 167, 176, 189

Ulysses (Tennyson), 18, 49, 78, 80, 85, 90

Use of Poetry and the Use of Criticism (Eliot), 177

Valediction, Forbidding Mourning (Donne), 157, 166
Venus and Adonis, 189
Via media, 193
Virgil, 19–20, 26, 28, 73, 76, 86, 138, 147–8, 154–5, 158, 169, 183–9
Virgin Mary, The, 13, 77, 82, 86, 92, 97, 109–14, 136, 167, 170, 175, 178, 180–1, 193

War in Heaven, 51, 162
Waste Land, The (Eliot), 2, 13 n., 25, 29, 32, 33, 49, 56 n., 71, 142, 144, 167, 175, 188
Webster, John, 142
Weston, Jessie, 33
West Wind, Ode to the (Shelley), 99, 112, 143
What is a Classic? (Eliot), 187
Whitman, Walt, 81, 113
Whittington, Dick, 10 n.
Williams, Charles, 111–12, 170
Wordsworth, William, 14
World War, First, 143, 193
World War, Second, 113, 138, 163